REMEMBERING DEXTER
MEMORIES OF A VERY SPECIAL BIRD-LOVING DOG

Book 5
in the Family of Rescue Dogs Series

BRIAN L. PORTER

Dedicated with love to the memory of Dexter
1st November 2007 – 8th June 2019

INTRODUCTION

This is the fifth book in my Family of Rescue Dogs series, and for the first time, features one of our dogs who is no longer with us. Sadly, Dexter passed away just two weeks ago. Though I had planned to make Dylan the subject of the next book in the series, such was the response to our loss of this special boy, on Facebook, with messages of sympathy, flowers and gifts sent to our home in his memory, that when I asked you, the readers, whose story you would like me to tell next, your answer was unanimous. You said DEXTER.

So, this is Dexter's story, one I hope you'll enjoy as much as the previous books in the series. Even though he is no longer with us, this is not a sad story. Far from it, Dexter's life with us was a happy time for us all, and I can honestly say that he was a very special boy, as you'll discover as you read about our very special 'bird-dog', affectionately known in the house, as Dexter-doo, or Mr. D!

ACKNOWLEDGMENTS

Usually, I would put the acknowledgements towards the end of the book. This time, however, I have deliberately changed the format, as there are certain people whose names deserve a mention, sooner rather than later.

A big thank you has to go to Rebecca Aldren and the vets, nurses and ancillary staff, at Vets 4 Pets, at Wheatley in Doncaster. In particular, I will always be grateful to Ximo Huertas Montón. In case the name doesn't give you a clue, Ximo is Spanish. For the last eighteen months he has been Dexter's vet, and Ximo, (pronounced Cheemo), couldn't have done more for Dexter. He treated him, not just on a professional level but also with compassion and a love for Dexter that bordered on being above and beyond the call of duty. Dexter trusted him as I did and was always pleased to see him on our many visits to the surgery. More of Ximo later in the book.

My thanks also to my dear friend Kath Bradbury. Kath's instant compassion and kindness when she learned of Dexter's passing touched us deeply and we will always be grateful to her, as we will to my friend and fellow author, Linda Lindsay, who reacted in a similar way and who was there for us when the grief was new and very raw.

Thanks to Debbie Poole. Not only is Debbie my chief researcher and proof reader for my Mersey Mystery series of novels, she's a great friend and was a terrific support when we lost Dexter. Thank you Deb, as always for proof-reading this book, which was quite an emotional trial for me to write and I know you were there were for me at all times.

To everyone who sent cards and messages of condolence, Juliet and I send our gratitude. Although we have lost Dexter, your actions have shown us that there are people out there who really do care about the feelings of others, especially in times of loss. In some ways you have helped to turn Dexter's loss into a celebration of his life, something I'm very grateful for.

Thanks also to everyone at the Facebook Group, Bully Lovers & Friends, for your constant interest, love and support during Dexter's final year.

This book is also intended to be a celebration of Dexter's life, so without further ado, let's embark on Dexter's journey.

1

SUMMER 2009

IT WAS A LOVELY, sunny summer's day, and like many families, we were trying to decide what to do with our Sunday afternoon.

"Can we go to the dog place?" Victoria my youngest stepdaughter asked.

Two weeks previously, we'd adopted our latest rescue dog, a beautiful brindle greyhound/lurcher we'd named Sophie, from the dog pound, situated about 15 miles from our home. Located out of town in the countryside, it was a pleasant location and a nice little run out in the car, so we agreed to pay them another visit. The girls, at that time aged nine and ten, wanted to take Sophie with us, but we convinced them that wasn't a good idea. Sophie might think we were taking her back there, and that wouldn't do at all. We'd take our 'pack leader' Tilly, the little cross breed terrier blessed with incredible intelligence and ability on the agility course, and who was learning search and rescue techniques at dog training. She loved car rides so it would be a little treat for her.

So, after lunch, we set off in the car and duly arrived at the pound about half an hour later. As soon as we got out of the car in the car park located outside the gates of the dog pound, we could hear the sounds of multiple dogs barking from within. They all wanted a home and were letting the world know it.

We were greeted warmly by the staff in the office, as they knew us well enough by that time. We'd already adopted a few dogs from them, and we were no strangers to the place.

"Back again," Louise asked as we smiled as if to say, "*We didn't have a choice in the matter.*"

"Just thought we'd have a look around," I replied. "Sophie is doing really well, so we decided we might find another new friend."

"You can't keep away from the place," Louise laughed, and she was right!

The layout of the kennels at the pound was basically a large rectangle with dog pens around the perimeter and another central building housing a further number of pens. Juliet and Victoria set off to the right, I went to look in the central building, and Rebecca aged ten, set off on her own to the left. After a few minutes of talking to various dogs through the bars of their pens, and wanting to adopt them all if I could have, Rebecca entered the building and called to me to come and look at something.

"You've got to see this dog," she said, and she took my hand to pull me in the desired direction. At the far end of the courtyard, two pens from the end of the row, she pointed to a dog. Because of the way the place was built, not a lot of natural sunlight entered the dog pens, depending on the sun's position in the sky. Here, I saw the dog Rebecca wanted me to look at. Lying at the front of its pen in a tiny triangle of sunshine, was a medium sized black dog. That wasn't the remarkable thing about it, however, as all dogs love lying in the sun. What was amazing about this particular dog, was the fact that he'd dragged his blanket from his bed in the stall at the rear of his pen to the sunny spot at the front, beside the bars. *Clever dog*, I thought.

"Hello there," I said to the dog, "Are you a clever dog, then?"

As if he understood my question, his tail began wagging, as if to confirm a positive reply.

"Can we have him, please?" Rebecca asked.

"Whoa there, wait a minute," I replied. "We only came to have a look around."

Of course, I was lying. We all knew that if we found a suitable dog, we'd be adopting another rescue. Juliet and I just hadn't put that thought into words.

"Oh, please can we have him? Look he's got white socks on," Rebecca pleaded.

"We'll go find your Mum and Victoria," I said. "They're looking around too, don't forget."

Looking a little crestfallen, Rebecca trudged along behind me as I went to find the others. A minute later we found them on the other side of the courtyard-shaped kennels, looking at a little terrier in a pen, together with another slightly larger cross-breed.

"Mummy, pleeease, come and look at the dog I found," Rebecca said as soon as were within earshot.

"What sort of dog?" Juliet asked.

"Looks like a Labrador, I replied."

Juliet and Victoria duly followed Rebecca and I to the far end of the kennels, where we'd seen the black dog.

"See how clever he is," I said, suddenly feeling the need to put a good word in for him. "Look how he's dragged his blanket into that little patch of sunlight in the corner." Juliet called to the dog, who now stood up and for the first time, revealed his beautiful white chest markings, which went nicely with his white socks, that I now saw only applied to his front paws. His back legs were all black.

Juliet agreed that he certainly seemed intelligent, but wanted to look round all the other dogs before making any enquiries about him. We spent about twenty minutes wandering around, looking at a sea of hopeful faces, wagging tails, and a few sad looking dogs who seemed to have 'lost their wag' and who just stood at the bars of their pens, looking out on a world that seemed to have abandoned them. Every time we visited the Pound, I would get a lump in my throat and I would wish we could adopt them all and give them a loving home for ever. Realistically, that wasn't possible of course, and I knew it, and the best we could do was to give a home to however many we could fit into our home.

Finally, we got to the end of the last row of pens, and we stood together to hold a quick family conference. The girls, of course, had already made up their minds. They wanted the black dog, sitting in the sun. Juliet and I agreed he was a very handsome dog, and that, depending on his temperament, he might fit in nicely with our little family of rescue dogs. It was time to go and talk to Louise in the office.

"See anything that takes your fancy?" were Louise's first words when we walked into the office.

"Possibly," Juliet did the talking. "What can you tell us about the black Labrador-looking dog in number XXX?"

(After all these years I can't recall the kennel number)

Without hesitation, Louise replied, "Oh, you mean Dexter?"

"He's got a name?" I asked, as it was unusual for the dogs at the pound to have names. They were usually strays or abandoned dogs with no collars or I.D. tags.

"He has," she replied. "He's even microchipped. But, he's got a bit of a story."

I leaned on the tall counter in the office and waited for Louise to go on. I was worried that there would be a reason that would make Dexter a bit of an adoption risk.

"Is there something wrong with him?" Juliet voiced our concerns.

"Not a thing," said Louise. "It's a sad tale really. Someone was driving along the motorway one day, quite recently, and suddenly saw a car up ahead open one of its doors, and a dog was literally thrown from the car onto the motorway. As it was travelling at about 60 mph, the poor dog hit the tarmac with some force and rolled over and over until it came to a halt on the hard shoulder. Luckily, there was no other traffic following the car, or he could have been hit and killed. The person who witnessed it, quickly applied the brakes and pulled onto the hard shoulder. They were too far behind to get the number of the car that threw him out, which quickly accelerated away, and was lost to sight in no time. They checked the poor dog, as best as they could, then gently loaded him into their car and drove him to the next town, luckily only a few miles down the road. They found a vet, told him what had happened, and left the dog in his care, after leaving him with a short, written statement for him to give to the authorities. The vet treated the poor dog, and scanned him and found a microchip. Because of the circumstances, the vet called the dog wardens. He wasn't keen on tracking down the person to whom Dexter was registered. Miraculously, Dexter wasn't seriously injured. He had suffered severe bruising, internal and external, but the prognosis for his future was good. The wardens of course brought him to us after he'd spent a night recuperating at the vets, and we phoned the name and number that the microchip was registered to. This was where things got a little murky. The person they spoke to said they were no longer the dog's owner. They said they'd sold him to someone but they didn't have a name and address for the new owner. They said they didn't want the dog and we could keep him."

"That sounds a real cock and bull story," I said, angrily. "I bet it was them that dumped him, because they just didn't want him."

"I think so too," said Louise, "but there's no way we can prove it, and as far as we're concerned, the dog comes first, no matter what."

"Of course it does," I said. I was really angry at the thought of what someone had done to Dexter. It was one of the most cruel and heartless acts I'd ever heard of. What if there'd been a large container truck or just a fast-moving car coming along when they threw him from the car? Not only would Dexter have been killed but the occupants of the following vehicle could have been seriously hurt or killed.

Juliet looked at me. I could tell she had a certain look in her eyes, and I kind of knew where this was all going.

"Can we take him for a little walk with Tilly?" I asked. "Just to see how he reacts to other dogs."

"'Course you can," Louise smiled at me. "You know where to go by now."

She was referring to a footpath that ran alongside a field on the other side of the road from where the Pound was located. It was quiet and peaceful there; the ideal place to walk a potentially nervous dog. She asked us to wait a minute while she went and brought Dexter to us. When she returned with him, I must admit, he was even better looking than he'd appeared at first sight, stuck in that pen, behind bars. His coat was sleek and shiny and he held his head up, proud as can be. When he saw us, his tail started wagging. He'd obviously remembered us from a few minutes earlier, and seemed to know he was going for a walk.

I held the lead as we walked out of the main gate and Juliet went to our car to get Tilly. The first hurdle was quickly cleared, as Tilly met Dexter for the first time. Despite him being twice her size, she walked up to him with a wagging tail, and Dexter wagged his, and they were the best of friends in about thirty seconds.

After crossing the busy main road, we walked along the grass verge for a few yards till we came to the entrance to the field, and the footpath. As we walked along beside the field with the afternoon sun shining all around, without a cloud in the sky, the sound of the vehicles on the road faded into the distance, and we could have been miles from civilisation.

Dexter walked like a dream on the lead. He walked by my side, while Tilly walked with Juliet, just behind us. Tilly wanted to catch up and play with her new friend, but we wanted to see how Dexter behaved first. After ten minutes we decided to change places, so we swapped dogs and Juliet moved to the front with Dexter and me and Tilly now brought up the rear. This was a good test for Dexter. Would he pull to try and catch up to Tilly? Would he want to assert himself by taking the lead again? We needn't have worried.

"What do you think then, girls?" I asked, and both Rebecca and Victoria lost no time in chorusing, "Can we have him, please?"

Juliet and I agreed that we could see no reason not to add Dexter to our family, but just to make sure, we gave him one last, important test. We wanted to see how he behaved at rest, so, we all sat on the grass at the side of the path. Tilly quickly stretched out and lay on the grass, enjoying the chance to lie in the sun. Dexter seemed a little unsure of himself at first, but as Juliet stroked his head, and gently told him to 'sit' as I did the same with Tilly, he promptly sat, and she stroked his head and then his back, and he relaxed completely.

The first walk with Dexter

The next thing we knew, he was lying by her side, enjoying the sun on his fur, and actually began falling asleep. He was so laid back, we couldn't help smiling. The girls came to him and knelt by his side, loving him with strokes and cuddles. They quite liked the idea of having a dog they could really put their arms round and hug and cuddle. We needn't have had any worries about how he would react to the children. He just adored all the attention they were lavishing on him, and was giving lots of licks in return. This was a dog you just couldn't help loving and our minds were made up that Dexter was going to be ours.

By now, we'd been out on our 'short' walk for over half an hour.

"Louise will think we've run off with him," I joked, as we began a slow walk back to the Pound.

"I take it everything went well, then," Louise smiled as we walked back into the office with Dexter, after putting Tilly in the car first.

"You'd better get the paperwork done, Louise. Dexter's got a new home," I said.

"Can we pick him up tomorrow?" Juliet asked. "We need to get him a bed, bowl, toys and all the usual stuff before we can take him home."

"Of course you can," Louise confirmed that was okay. "We'll give him a bath in the morning for you, so he'll smell a bit sweeter."

"Thanks, Louise. That'll be a big help," Juliet said, impressed with the service. "He doesn't really smell bad or anything."

"I know, but he's such a lovely boy. He deserves to leave here looking and smelling great," Louise smiled as she spoke.

"That's really good of you," I said. "I think you've got a bit of a soft spot for this young fella, haven't you?"

"You could say that," she replied.

"We forgot to ask, do you know how old he is?" Juliet asked, always the sensible one.

"Oh yes, of course, he's about eighteen months old, according to the information we got when we checked his chip."

"So he's not much more than a baby, really. I just can't work out why anyone would just throw him from a moving car," I said, still angry at what had been done to him.

"We have a theory about that," Louise turned serious for a minute. "He's a Labrador/Staffy Crossbreed and we think

9

someone wanted him to be a guard dog or perhaps a fighter, and he's so placid and laid back, he just didn't measure up to their expectations, so they just got rid of him."

"I'll never understand people," Juliet said. "Why couldn't they just have handed him in to a dog sanctuary, or even to a place like this? There are plenty of places that will take and rehome unwanted dogs."

"Your guess is as good as mine," Louise replied. "Some of the things we see and hear in this place, you wouldn't believe."

"I'm sure," I agreed. "I don't think we could put up with some of the heartbreaking sights you must see"

We continued to interact with Dexter while Louise completed the adoption paperwork. Finally, she finished what she had to do, and after I handed over a deposit, (I'd pay the balance when I collected him the next day), I signed on the dotted line, and then, apart from that last payment being needed, Dexter was, to all intents and purposes, ours!

Dexter actually looked quite sad as Louise led him away back to his lonely pen. We tried to reassure him that it was just for one last night. Did he understand what we were saying? I'd like to think so. At least his tail was wagging as he disappeared around the corner out of our sight.

We were all excited on the drive home. We hadn't really intended to adopt another dog when we left home that afternoon, but, now that we'd found Dexter, we couldn't wait for Monday to come around.

That evening, time seemed to drag, and bedtime couldn't come around soon enough. Juliet and I prepared a little shopping list for Dexter. He would need a nice comfy bed, a feeding bowl, a good quality collar and lead, and a couple of toys. I'd have to do a pretty fast shopping trip in the morning so that I'd be free to go and collect Dexter when they opened at noon on Monday.

For now, though, we were all relieved when bedtime approached, and we could let the dogs out for the last time of the day. They were all soon tucked up in their beds, contented snoring emanating from a couple of them, and it wasn't long before we climbed the stairs and doing our best to get a good night's sleep. Tomorrow promised to be a busy day!

2

THE HOMECOMING

WE WOKE up bright and early as usual the following morning. We're always up and about from 5.30 am as there's a lot to do, feeding the dogs, letting them out and clearing up after them, before Juliet and I get the time to use the bathroom, and get ourselves ready for the day ahead.

I would usually set off on the first walk of the day soon after 7 am and on my return, Juliet would take her first group, and so on, until they were all walked. Nothing was any different that morning, except for the air of excitement and anticipation that hung over us all, at the prospect of our new arrival. I'd agreed to take Rebecca and Victoria with me to the Dog Pound to collect Dexter, (the girls were on summer holiday from school), along with Tilly, who provide a familiar face for him while travelling in the car.

The sun was shining again that morning, and before we could even think about going to collect our new boy, I had another important task to fulfil. As soon as the dog walks were completed, I relaxed long enough to enjoy a mug of coffee, and then, armed with my wallet and instructions from Juliet, (I sometimes do as I'm told), I set off for the pet superstore, about three miles away from our home.

Once there, I spent a few minutes selecting a new bed for Dexter, a lovely padded mattress for him. and a large size black collar with white paw prints on it, a matching lead, and a new feeding bowl. Now came the next, important acquisition, toys!

As most dog owners know, toys can play an important role in a dog's life. Pick the right one, and he or she will take to it and spend hours playfully enjoying themselves with it. As we didn't really know Dexter, I was sort of 'shooting in the dark' when it came to choosing toys for him. Of course, whatever I selected, I had to be aware that the other dogs would share my choice, and the one thing I had to avoid was...squeaky toys!

We'd already learned that when you have a pack of dogs, squeaky toys can be a source of conflict among the dogs. When one dog has the toy, and makes it squeak, one or more of the other dogs instantly make a bee-line for them and attempt to steal the toy for themselves. In other words, the next thing you know, you have a dog fight on your hands, as, like squabbling children in a playground, they dive in, teeth bared, trying to claim the toy. In such cases, they never really hurt each other and the only real damage would be to the toy! When we'd eventually manage to separate the furry monsters, the toy would usually be in tatters, the squeak destroyed, and pieces of dog toy strewn around the house or garden.

Now, you'll understand why this was an important, perhaps vital job, if I were to satisfy Dexter's play urges and at the same time avoid potential conflict in the pack, and of course, wasting my money on something that wouldn't last more than ten minutes!

I spent more than ten minutes searching through the store's selection of dog toys, looking for suitable 'squeak-less' toys, eventually settling on what resembled a large, hard plastic teething ring, a special non-squeak chicken and a couple of tough-looking tug toys he could share with the other dogs. I knew from past experience that the tug toys wouldn't last long, but the dogs would have some fun with them, and they wouldn't break the bank when it came to buying replacements.

Dog shopping done, I loaded everything into the dog bed, which made a good receptacle for carrying everything to the car. I was soon back home, and much to my relief, Juliet approved of my choices. I'd negotiated a major hurdle there, and it would soon be time to leave for the Pound. So, Rebecca, Victoria and I had an early lunch, and before we knew it, the time had come to go and collect our new adoptee. The Dog Pound opened to the public at noon, and the girls were anxious to collect Dexter as soon as they opened, (Okay, I admit it, so was I), so to make sure we were there in time, we loaded Tilly in the car, and left home just before 11.30 am. Tilly was of course, excited. She loved car journeys, as they usually meant something pleasurable for her at the end of them.

We made good time on our journey, and pulled into car park outside the gates of the Pound at about five minutes to twelve. Perfect timing! We got out of the car, and let Tilly out, and walked her around for a couple of minutes so she could do what a dog has to do, then she had to go back into the car when Kath, one of the staff, arrived to open up.

Seeing us standing there, with me holding Dexter's new collar and lead, waiting for her to open up, she smiled a greeting, saying, "You're keen aren't you? Dexter's all ready and waiting for you. Come on in and we'll bring him to the office for you."

"Thanks, Kath," I replied. "Yes, we couldn't wait to get here today."

She laughed. She knew us only too well, and probably

wasn't a bit surprised to see us standing outside the gates, waiting for her to open up.

The girls and I waited in the office for a couple of minutes, chatting with Louise, who told us she had personally given Dexter a bath that morning, and that he seemed to love it."

"Thank you for doing that for us, Louise," I said, and I meant it. I knew it wasn't something they did for everybody.

The door to the office opened, and in walked Kath with our boy. I'd wondered if Dexter would remember us from the previous day, and I shouldn't have worried. As soon as he saw us his tail began wagging furiously, so much so that his entire back end seemed to wag with it!

"He looks really happy to see you," Louise commented.

"He does, doesn't he?" I laughed as I made a fuss of him.

Kath held her hand out and I passed her his new collar, which she fastened round his neck, and then clipped his new lead on. Now he looked like a dog that belonged to somebody. The only thing he was lacking was an identity tag, but I'd ordered a nice stainless steel tag that morning which would be engraved with his details, and delivered within three days.

The girls made a big fuss of Dexter and continued to keep him company while I dealt with the final bits of paperwork that would confirm his adoption. I paid the balance of the adoption fee and Louise handed over his adoption certificate, and his vaccination card. Regardless of whether they had a dog's health records, the Pound always started their dogs off with fresh vaccinations. Their vet administered the first vaccination and it was up to the new owner to obtain the second one two weeks later. Dexter's card showed their vet had given him his first jab that morning, so we had a fortnight before he'd need his second one.

Everything completed, both Louise and Kath gave Dexter a big hug and a cuddle and as quickly as that, he was ours, and we walked out of the gates, to our car, where Tilly could see us coming, paws up at the window, her tail wagging furiously. As I lifted the tailgate of our Mondeo Estate car, I was astounded when, without being told to, Dexter just jumped into the car, as if to say, *"You're not going without me."* Probably the first words I said to him now that he was officially ours, and which would be repeated many times in the coming years, were, "Good boy, Dexter."

Tilly clearly remembered him from the previous day and welcomed him with more tail wagging, and she was very excited as we drove away from the Dog Pound, jumping up and down at her new friend, who didn't seem the least bit bothered by the fussy, feisty little terrier. In fact, by glancing periodically in the rear-view mirror, I could see Dexter was looking through the rear windows, showing a lot of interest in his surroundings as we travelled along. The girls were also giving me a running commentary on what the two dogs were doing in the back.

In what seemed no time at all, we arrived at our home and Juliet was standing in the front garden, waiting to welcome Dexter to his new home. I opened the tailgate and Tilly, as usual leaped from the car, to be followed, surprisingly, by Dexter, who just assumed that what Tilly did, he had to do, too. I grabbed a hold of Tilly's lead, and one of the girls got a hold of Dexter's, and we all walked through the gate into the front garden.

"Hello Dexter," Juliet greeted him, with a hug and lots of strokes. She was rewarded by mega tail wags and a big sloppy doggie kiss. She laughed with delight. Dexter looked so happy, as if he sensed he was in his new, forever home, where he was safe and loved. He hadn't even come into the house yet, but we all knew, as he and Tilly bounced around on the front garden, and before he'd met the rest of our dogs, Dexter was home!

3

HOME

AFTER A COUPLE of minutes frolicking in the front garden, it was time to introduce Dexter to the rest of our family of rescue dogs. We went through the side gate and took Dexter through to the back garden, allowing him the chance to have a roam around his new territory in peace for a minute. He duly had a good sniff around and of course, took the first step towards claiming it as his new home by cocking his leg up against a couple of the bushes at the bottom of the garden. Most of the garden area is paved. We'd had it done to allow easy cleaning up after the dogs, though we had an area at furthest from the house where we had a number of plants and shrubs growing in large pots, and our bird table.

Now came the most important part of the day. While I stayed outside with Dexter and Tilly, Juliet and the girls went indoors and after going through the usual greeting ritual, (lots of jumping, licking and hugs), they allowed the dogs out, a couple at a time to meet the new arrival. We've found this to be the ideal way to introduce new dogs to the family. A gradual introduction is far better than allowing the whole pack out at once, which would probably result in the newcomer becoming scared and overwhelmed and could, conceivably lead to fighting, to be avoided at all costs.

The introductions went without a hitch and over the next half hour, Dexter got to know his new pack mates. There was no hint of animosity, either from Dexter or any of our existing pack, and we were delighted that Dexter had been so readily accepted. Now came the time to show him the house.

As the other dogs seemed completely at ease with him, we simply walked into the house and Dexter followed us, interested in where we were going. The other dogs mostly stayed in the garden, just a couple being bothered to join us. Dexter was so good, he walked around the kitchen, exploring all the dog beds and the water bowls, stopping for a quick drink before continuing his exploration. We opened the door to the hall and he just wandered through to the hall and then through the door to the lounge. Another two minutes were spent as he checked it out and then without being told, he walked back to the kitchen. We then showed him the nice new bed I'd bought him that morning.

"Dexter's bed," I said pointing to it and patting the mattress to indicate to him that it was his. To entice him into trying it out, Juliet took the large ring I'd bought him from a bag on the table and put it in the bed. That did it. He had to check it out, didn't he?

He climbed into the bed, and instantly picked up the teething ring, as I called it, sat down on his nice soft mattress and began to chew on it.

"I think he likes it," said Juliet.

"I think you're right," I agreed.

Dexter chewed on it for a minute or so, and then, with the big ring still held firmly in his jaws, he lay down and promptly fell asleep. "How's that for making himself at home?" I smiled to see him so at home. He'd been in the house less than an hour and there he was, snoozing quite contentedly, without a care in the world. "That's so good to see. It's as if he knows he's safe and loved now," Juliet agreed with me. "Looking at him, you'd think he'd been here all his life."

The girls were both amazed at how well Dexter had made himself at home and one of them, I'm not sure who, asked if we would be taking him for a walk later in the afternoon. As the other dogs wandered in and out of the kitchen, occasionally stopping to sniff at the newcomer in their midst, and then totally ignoring him, Juliet smiled and replied,

"I don't see why not, but we can't let him off the lead, remember."

It was one of the rules attached to the terms of adoptions from the Dog Pound, that the new owners agreed to keep their new dog on a lead while walking for the first two weeks, at least. This gave the dog a chance to bond with his or her new family, and by the time the dog was allowed to walk off-lead, there was less chance of him running away and disappearing over the horizon. Remember that rule, as we'll come back to it a little later.

Sure enough, the time for afternoon walks soon arrived. Usually, we'd split the dogs up into two, with Juliet and Rebecca taking half, and Victoria and I waiting at home until they returned, before we set off with the other half. Today, though we decided to make an exception, and the four of us would share the dogs between us, and we'd all go at once for a change.

We soon had the dogs on their leads, and with an ample supply of dog treats in our pockets and a couple of tennis balls, our little band of furry friends and the four of us set off, heading for the playing field not far from where we lived. As Dexter already knew Tilly, he walked with me and her, with the rest of the dogs shared between Juliet, Rebecca and Victoria.

The only real worry we had was how Dexter would react to any dogs we might meet on the field. He'd shown himself to be friendly enough, but would that extend to a walk with the whole pack? We needn't have worried. Dexter was so laid back on his walk, that I'd have sworn he hardly noticed the dogs we came into contact with. Most of them were owned by friends of ours, and as we hadn't told anyone we were getting another dog, (we didn't know ourselves until the day before), they were surprised to see a new face among our pack, and were excited and interested to meet him and were full of questions about him.

Without exception, they were all horrified when we told them what we knew of his background and nobody could understand how anyone could be cruel as to throw a dog from a moving car, especially at high speed on a motorway. Consequently, they all made a big fuss of Dexter, and their dogs all said hello in typical doggie fashion, with much sniffing and tail wagging. This led us to our first negative discovery about Dexter. He wasn't keen on having his bottom sniffed! After he'd growled at the first two dogs who tried to indulge in this traditional dog 'getting to know you' behaviour, we made sure to tell everyone not to allow their dogs to sniff around his rear end. All in all, however, it was a successful first walk and Dexter certainly seemed to enjoy himself. Perhaps, we thought, he'll get over his sniffing negativity in time. After all, it was his first day in a totally new environment and it was probably a massively traumatic experience for him.

One thing became clear from that first walk. Dexter loved being outdoors. He loved exploring the bushes and trees that surrounded the playing field, and was totally at ease walking by my side. It was proving a great first day so far. Soon, it was time for us all to head for home. It was almost feeding time for the dogs, and as soon as we got home, we began preparing the meals for all our pack.

Though some of our dogs became quite excited at tea time, Dexter just sat and waited patiently as Juliet made his tea up, and when he was presented with his bowl, he didn't try to grab, or jump up, or exhibit any bad manners. He waited until Juliet put his bowl down in front of him and said "Tea, Dexter, good boy," and he promptly stepped forward and proceeded to eat his meal, slowly, no rushing or gulping it down. He really enjoyed his food, and in fact seemed to relish it so much, he was the last to finish.

"Well done Dexter," I said, and his tail wagged at the words of praise. As it was a warm, sunny evening, we allowed the dogs out in the garden after tea and most of them took advantage of the evening sunshine to lie on the outdoor rugs we provided for them and bask in the rays of the warm evening sun, with the clear blue sky above, and hardly a cloud in sight.

After the way we'd first seen him at the Dog Pound, it was hardly surprising when Dexter wandered out in to join them, and without hesitation lay down on his side and proceeded to fall asleep in the sun. He'd not even been with us a full day, but already, we felt confident that he was going to fit in perfectly as part of our family of rescue dogs.

That feeling was further reinforced when, without being told, Dexter walked across the kitchen to his bed, got in, and promptly began chewing on his giant teething ring. It was how I thought of it and was the way I always described it. It was so rewarding to see him lying contentedly in his bed, the ring in his mouth, seemingly without a care in the world. Just twenty-four hours ago, this beautiful dog had been locked in a cell-like 'kennel' with a hard, concrete floor and just a bed and a blanket for company. Now he had a new family, with doggie friends, is very own humans to love and care for him, his teething ring, and most importantly of all, Dexter had found his forever home!

When it came round to bedtime, we followed our usual routine, letting all the dogs out in the back garden for late-night wees and poos, and as always we didn't rush them, allowing them time to wander around the garden for a few minutes, before settling down for the night. I kept a close watch on them all; it was Dexter's first night with us, after all.

I wasn't in the least bit surprised when Dexter was the last to come in from the garden. He'd obviously been doing a bit more exploring of his new territory and when he eventually came in, I gave him a hug, and lots of strokes, repeated after I'd finished by Juliet, who said as she did every night before closing the kitchen door and turning the lights off, "Good night, doggies."

I finished off by saying "Goodnight Mr. Dexter," and just before the lights went out, I saw he was in bed, sort of cuddling up with his teething ring. I got the feeling Dexter had never had any toys of his own before, which I related to Juliet when we got to bed.

"Poor little Dexter," she said and then, "Well, he won't go without toys from now on, will he?"

"There's no chance of that," I said. "That dog can have all the toys he wants if it makes him happy. Let's make sure he can forget the bad start he's had in life, and give him some happiness."

"And love," Juliet said, "Lots and lots of love."

"Mmmm," I dreamily agreed as I drifted off to sleep. It had, after all, been a long and exciting day for all of us, and Dexter too.

New home, new bed

4

DEXTER THE BULLET TRAIN

WHEN WE WOKE the following morning, after Dexter's first night in our home, we were pleased to find no accidents waiting for us and we hoped that was a sign that Dexter was house trained. Perhaps his previous owner had done something right with him.

After Juliet had drunk her morning cup of tea, and I'd finished my first coffee of the day, (I'm something of a coffee addict in the mornings), and we'd let all the dogs out in the back garden to relieve themselves, it was time for breakfast. We know that some dogs are fed once a day, others twice, and we had no idea which group Dexter fell in to. All our dogs were used to being fed twice a day, a small meal for breakfast and their main meal later in the day, after everyone had been for their afternoon walks.

Juliet and I placed all the dog bowls out and most of the dogs went to their bowls and hungrily ate their breakfast, apart from one or two who would invariably decide to stay in their beds until everyone had eaten and would then get up to eat theirs. Dexter wasted no time in turning up for his. He soon cleared his bowl and we were sure he'd have no trouble fitting into the twice a day routine. Our only worry when we adopted a new dog was whether they would take time to adjust to a change of food. Sometimes, a total change of diet can lead to temporary tummy and bowel trouble. Thankfully, this problem never affected Dexter, who loved his food, but unlike some dogs, who tried to set a world record for clearing a bowl of food every meal time, Dexter never rushed his food, and as would become his habit, ate like he was savouring every mouthful.

From the beginning, Dexter loved going for his walks. Trouble was, everyone wanted to take him! So we worked it out that we would share him, with Juliet and Rebecca taking him in the morning and Victoria and I taking him in the afternoon. He was such a pleasure to take for a walk. He never pulled, walked at whatever pace we did, with his head held proudly and his long tail held straight out at the rear, with the occasional wag to let us know he was enjoying himself. Dexter loved exploring while he was out for a walk and we all had to learn a certain degree of patience, as he would stop to investigate a sight or sound in the hedgerows around the playing field or by the road-side, and when we took him in the local wood...have you any idea just how many hundreds of smells and scents are lurking in those trees and bushes to attract a passing dog? We some-times had to get quite firm with Dexter or we'd have been stuck in that wood all day and night, until they sent search parties out to find us.

The problem was, we couldn't let him off the lead yet, so we had to stop when he stopped and as he was quite a strong dog, if one of the girls was holding his lead, they stood a good chance of being unexpectedly dragged under a bush if Dexter caught a hint of something particularly smelly! We couldn't wait for him to have his second vaccinations, which would coincide with the time when we should, theoretically be able to safely let him run free.

Oops, we got that wrong. We met our first problem with Dexter a day or two after we'd visited the vet for his jab, and I had him thoroughly checked over by the vet at the time as it was his first visit, a sort of 'doggie M.O.T. (for my American readers, an M.O.T test is a regular safety test carried out on cars over three years old, every year to determine their roadworthiness). Without an M.O.T certificate it's illegal to drive a car on British roads. I was pleased when our vet pronounced Dexter fully fit in every department. He commented on Dexter's beautiful sleek coat, and after I'd told him Dexter's history, he reassured me that he could find no residual effects of his close call on the motorway.

Returning to this particular walk I mentioned, it was the weekend so we decided that we'd take the dogs out in two big walks, with all four of us going with half the pack first of all, then the second half after we'd completed the first walk. The first walk went off without a hitch, as we took most of the smaller dogs on this walk, who were all well trained and presented no problems when allowed to run free. The same applied to the 'second team' we took out, apart from the one unknown quantity...Dexter.

Because of the slightly different format to these two walks, we'd set off a lot earlier than usual to give us plenty of time to let all the dogs have a good run and play. This proved to be a wise decision as on the second walk things went slightly wrong. The second walk was going to plan, as we walked all the dogs round the perimeter of the playing field once and then decided it was okay to let the dogs loose for a run. Dexter had been with us for two weeks, and we certainly believed he'd bonded with us by this time. He was obedient and really quite submissive at home and had never caused any of us any problems on his twice a day lead walks. So, just to be on the safe side, Juliet and I scanned the playing field for other dogs, not one was in sight.

We let Tilly, Sophie, Molly and Charlie off their leads first and the girls proceeded to run around and play with them, thinking that this would give Dexter a good idea of the purpose of 'doggie playtime'. Wrong!

As soon as Juliet unclipped Dexter's lead from his collar, he took a good look all around him and then...Whoosh, he was off! He was like a bullet train as he sped across the field. If I hadn't seen it with my own eyes, I'd never have believed he could run so fast.

"Dexter!" I shouted...no response.

"Dexter! Come here!" Juliet shouted...no response.

"Dexter, please come back," the two girls called in unison as Dexter's dwindling shape drew nearer and nearer the entrance to the lane that ran adjacent to the local junior school. Known locally as 'Piggy Lane' (because over fifty years ago a local farmer had built pig sties along this rough track that was never a proper road, and the name lives on to this day), Dexter was soon lost from sight among the bushes and hedgerows that lined the lane. There was also an old dried ditch that ran along one side of the lane, where, as children, we used to build dens and hideouts during the long hot summers of our youth. Nowadays, however, it was filled with all manner of rocks, rubble and discarded rubbish and we were afraid that if Dexter entered it, he could easily hurt himself badly.

"Damn it," I blasphemed as we tried to get all the other dogs to come back so we could clip them on their leads and go in search of the runaway. It took us about a minute to gather all the dogs in and attach their leads and all this time we were scanning our surroundings in the hope of catching sight of Dexter. Our biggest worry was that he'd keep going until he reached the end of Piggy Lane, which eventually petered out as it joined the side verge of a busy road. If Dexter took that route, he was in serious danger of being hit by a car or something larger, and potentially fatally.

"We've got to find him, Mummy," Victoria said, obviously upset and worried.

"Why did he run away?" Rebecca asked, worry etched into her young face.

"I don't know, perhaps he's just exploring," Juliet replied and then, far away in the distance, I caught sight of him.

"Look, there," I pointed, and all eyes turned to follow the direction of my finger.

Sure enough, Dexter was in the rough grass that bordered Piggy Lane, around the area where the pig sties once stood. He was sort of bouncing up and down, a result of the rough terrain and his own exuberance. Juliet and the girls called his name, but he was too far away for their voices to carry to him. Then, he suddenly vanished from view again, and worry crept into our minds once more. Which direction would he take? Further away from us, and into potential danger, or back in our direction and safety (if we could catch him)?

Suddenly, as if by magic, the black bullet train zoomed into view at the end of Piggy Lane where it joined the path by the school. He then made a ninety degree turn to his right, and gathering speed, headed right for us. We were all calling his name and encouraging him to keep coming towards us.

"Come on Dexter, good boy," I shouted and Juliet and the girls were shouting the same or similar encouragements to him. Boy, that dog was fast. Having caught sight of us, or was it his doggie friends, he now came at us in a straight line, like a torpedo heading for its target. We were all cheering him on as he drew nearer and nearer. Just when it seemed as if he was going to go rushing straight past us, Dexter applied the brakes. He appeared to go from top speed to full stop in less than a couple of seconds. He came to a halt, right in front of me, his tongue lolling out to one side and his tail wagging furiously. Then he sat, looking up at me, and it seemed as if he was waiting for me to say something. So I did.

"Good boy, Dexter," I said, stroking his head, and making a big, big, fuss of him. Now, you might think that was a strange thing to do to a dog who'd just run away and given us a fair few minutes of worry for his safety and whereabouts. But, just stop and think about it for a minute.

One important thing I learned whilst working with Brian the dog psychologist is that, if you shout at the dog, or worse still, smack him, as I know some people do in situations like this, what message are you sending to your dog? Run away and come back and you get told off, or beaten? If you want your dog to be loyal and to come back to you, no matter what, praise him when he comes back, make him feel you are pleased that he's returned to you. I guarantee he won't do it again, or, if he does, he won't be afraid to come back to you. You can always revert to training, as we knew we would have to, to ensure Dexter controlled his wanderlust, which is what we did, but more of that later.

For now, we were pleased our boy was back with us, and Dexter looked pleased with himself. I was sure that, in his mind, he'd simply been excited at being given the chance to run free, and had taken the opportunity to have a really good time, stretched his legs, and had then come back to us. Remember how we saw him from a distance, jumping up above the tall grass? I think he was actually doing that to get his bearings and making sure he could see us, and when he'd had a really good run, he came back to us, without realising he'd almost given us heart attacks from the worry. After all, Dexter was a dog, and he thought like a dog, not like a human!

We walked home, all together, with Dexter trotting beside

me, occasionally looking up at me as if to seek reassurance, which I gave gladly.

"Dexter's a good boy, aren't you? Yes, you are, you're a very good boy," and so on. Never once did I tell him off. He was just checking out his new territory, after all. The following day, Victoria and I took Dexter on the smaller playing field near our home, along with Tilly, Sophie, Charlie and Molly.

"Are we going to let him off again?" she asked me, with a hint of trepidation in her voice. I'm sure she secretly thought that Dexter would do a runner again, and perhaps be lost to us for ever, but I had a good feeling about our relationship, our bond with Dexter.

"We are, Victoria," I replied to her question. "We have to show him that we trust him, and just you watch, because I don't think Dexter will run away again."

Sure enough, a few minutes later, we were on the field, there was nobody else around and we let the dogs off their leads to play, Dexter included! Never once in the next half hour did Dexter give any hint that he might run away from us. He stayed pretty close, apart from going over to the edge of the playing field, where lots of shrubs and bushes grew wild, where he could explore and sniff and do whatever dogs do in such places.

In fact, for the rest of his life with us, Dexter never again did his bullet train impersonation. Praising him on his return that first day had clearly done the trick, cementing a bond of trust that worked both ways. Dexter trusted us, and I think he knew we trusted him.

Mr. 'D.'

5

LORD DEXTER

EARLIER IN THIS TALE, I mentioned training, and Juliet agreed with me that once he'd been fully vaccinated, we could think about taking Dexter to dog training classes. If you've read any of the previous books in this series, you'll know that Saturday afternoons were when the girls and I took some of the dogs to dog training, organised and run by my friend, Brian Gallagher, the canine psychologist.

We always attended, first of all, because it was great fun and a chance to meet and talk with other dog owners, and secondly, because Tilly was something of a star at dog agility, and was also learning (quite successfully), the skills of being a search and rescue dog. In addition to Tilly, we'd usually take three other dogs, and tried to make sure all the pack got a chance to attend. It was fun for the dogs, and they all enjoyed it.

We'd already introduced Sophie, our greyhound/lurcher, to the classes and as they got on so well together, we decided that Dexter could go along on the weeks we took Sophie. Saturday duly came around and after an early lunch, the girls and I got ready to go. We made sure we had plenty of treats to use as rewards. As training was a different discipline to the normal, everyday type of walk, I made sure the treats we used at dog training were something special for the dogs. Every week I bought a tin of hot-dog sausages and before leaving for the training session, I'd chop the hot-dogs up into small, bite-sized pieces and share them between me and the girls, so we'd all have a good supply when we got there. You'd be surprised how many treats you can get out of a single hot-dog sausage. Usually, by being careful, I could get 14 or 15 treats from one sausage, so it's easy for you to figure out how many treats we got from a tin of 6 of the tasty sausages.

Loaded up with our treats, water bottles and of course, the ultimate necessity, poo-bags, we set off for Dexter's first training session. He'd never shown any signs of aggression since we'd adopted him, but it never hurts to make sure of your new dog's temperament, (especially a rescue of unknown background and history), so we thought it wise to let Dexter socialise with as many new dogs as possible, and let him have some fun with the various dog games and exercises at the training session.

Brian, the trainer, and all the regulars were pleased to welcome our new addition and of course, everyone wanted to know his story. When I told them how he'd been callously thrown from a moving car, there were gasps of astonishment from some and expressions of anger from others who would have happily done some physical damage to his previous, heartless and cruel owner. They all made a big fuss of him and of Sophie, who was herself still a relative newcomer to the class. As for Dexter, he enjoyed all the fuss and cuddles he received from his new admirers, many of whom complimented us on his beautiful, shiny black coat. He also seemed to be quite at home with all the strange dogs, whom he was meeting for the first time. Sometimes, a dog can become a little overwhelmed the first time they are taken to the classes, by suddenly being surrounded by so many unknown dogs, which can often lead to a little fear aggression, but Dexter was unmoved by being suddenly placed in close proximity to so many dogs. He was definitely Mr. Laid Back!

Once the session began, everything seemed to go well at first. As always, we began with some basic obedience exercises. As we'd only had him a few weeks, Brian the trainer, (as opposed to Brian the owner, me of course), was impressed by his reactions to my voice, and his ability to sit, stay, and come to me on command. Recall is often the hardest thing for a new dog to learn, (remember the bullet train?), but Dexter was a star pupil and didn't put a paw wrong through these warm-up exercises.

Brian the trainer asked me if he had been so well behaved from the start or whether I'd been doing much training with him at home. I explained that from the first day, we'd worked on training him, and had concentrated on the basics and that it was obvious to Juliet and I that Dexter was a fast learner. I explained about his 'bullet train' episode and I was pleased when Brian agreed with my theory that he'd been simply happy to be allowed to run free and his actions when he seemed to be jumping up and down in the long grass suggested he was, as I'd thought, keeping an eye on us and in reality, we probably never really had a reason to worry, as he soon came back to us.

"That's easy for you to say," I told him. "You weren't left there on that field with four other dogs while the 'black flash' disappeared into the distance, wondering if that was the last you'd ever see of him."

"You never had a thing to worry about," he smiled. "I know you probably felt a few minutes of panic, but he certainly proved to you that you have a good bond with him already."

"I suppose you're right. He certainly seems to be a 'home

boy' sort of dog. He definitely loves the comforts of home and never needs telling twice to do something, well, not yet, anyway."

We moved on to the next part of the session, which was usually fun and funny. Fun, because most of the dogs loved flyball, and some were just so hopeless at it that we all had a laugh at their antics. I remember when our Tilly first tried it. Although, she was fast and could have been good at the sport, she just wouldn't give up the tennis ball. Once it was in her jaws, it stayed there, and everyone had a laugh at her antics when I tried to get her to give me that ball back.

Anyway, when it came to Dexter's turn to have a go, with me beside him for the first run, to guide him and show him what to do, we met the new, super stubborn Dexter. He wouldn't move! No matter how I tried to convince him that the idea of the game was to run to the end of the course, he just stood there, an immovable black lump of fur, (with a white chest of course). Victoria and Rebecca even went and stood at the other end of the course and tried calling him, jumping up and down and waving their arms furiously in an attempt to attract his attention, but he just stayed where he was, as still as a statue. By now, I was finding it rather amusing and the other owners were as well, and some were growing frustrated as their dogs were waiting for their turn. When I accepted defeat and turned to walk away from the flyball course, laughter rang out from the others, because, after playing statues for so long, Dexter was trotting along happily just behind me. If there hadn't been children present, I guarantee I would have used a few choice swear words at that point.

Instead, with a big smile on my face, I said, "Come on, Dexter, let's sit this one out eh? Maybe flyball just isn't your thing huh?"

The girls came back to join me, with our other dogs, and we

spent the next quarter of an hour happily relaxing and watching and occasionally laughing at the other dogs. It was a lovely sunny afternoon and warm, without being too hot for the dogs, but the next thing I knew, I looked to my side and there was Dexter, on his side, asleep and quietly snoring contentedly. I smiled to myself. Dexter was obviously completely bored by the whole business of flyball.

When the flyball session ended, the class moved on to Tilly's favourite part of the day...dog agility! Tilly absolutely loved agility training. She was so good at it that, eventually, she was able to negotiate the course without a handler. She was so fast that it looked as if her paws were barely touching the ground, and Brian, who times every dog on every run, was amazed when Tilly became the first dog to complete is course in under a minute, crossing the finish line in 58 seconds. On a course where the average dog did well to finish in 68 to 75 seconds, Brian was truly flabbergasted by Tilly's performance. A couple of weeks later, she repeated the performance, and then, a few weeks later, she knocked another second off her record, which was now 57 seconds. To the best of my knowledge, her record still stands to this day.

Tilly gets in a spot of training at home

On this day, as usual Tilly went first to show the others how to do it, then the others took turns. Sophie loved it, she was tall and rangy and very athletic. She liked the jumps especially. The rest of ours weren't very good at it but they always had a good go, and seemed to have fun. When it came to Dexter's turn to have a go, however, he made it quite clear that he wasn't really interested in the idea of running around and jumping over obstacles, going through tunnels and climbing and walking along a narrow plank. He wouldn't do a thing. He just stood there, with me holding his lead and trying to encourage him to trot along beside me to the first jump.

He looked up at me with a certain look that seemed to say, *"You must be joking."*

It was as if he considered himself too aristocratic to participate in such activities. In fact, one of the other owners, said, "Look at Lord Dexter. He won't join in with the peasants."

There was much laughter among the owners, and the name stuck for as long as he was a regular at the training sessions, with everyone calling him Lord Dexter.

Brian agreed that, like Flyball, agility training really wasn't Dexter's thing, and from then on, when we took him to dog training it was just for fun and socialising with the other dogs. The more energetic pursuits were definitely off the menu for Dexter. Lord knows what would happen when we had our once a month session in the large wood near the town's racecourse. How would he react to Search & Rescue training? I dreaded to think!

Every session ended with a half-hour of socialising, with all the dogs let off their leads to run around and enjoy themselves, and it gave us owners and kids a chance to interact, have a good chat, and swap dog stories and so on. All the dogs were happily running around, playing or just generally having a good time, and then we noticed Dexter and Sophie. Instead of running around, (who wants to get hot and sweaty anyway?), the two of them were like Lord and Lady Porter, calmly relaxing on the grass, watching the 'peasants' expending all that energy while they just took it easy. Dexter was showing himself to be quite a character, and everyone fell in love with him over the weeks we took him to dog training.

Of course, when we got home that day, Juliet was very interested to know how Dexter had done at his first training session.

"Let's put it this way," I replied. "He's never going to break any course records at agility, flyball is a big no, no, and the whole thing bored him so much that he lay down and fell asleep?"

She couldn't help herself and just like the people at the training session, she burst out laughing. She could just picture the whole scenario, and said, "Poor old Dexter. Did they try and make you join in with all those nasty exercises?"

Dexter just stood there wagging his tail, obviously thinking he'd been a really good boy, as Juliet stroked and cuddled him as if he'd just won the Olympic marathon.

His first day at training hadn't gone quite as planned, but it was fun, and we all had a good laugh!

"Let's you and me sit this one out, Dexter"

6

DEXTER IN LOVE?

DEXTER CERTAINLY DIDN'T TAKE LONG to settle into our home and our lives. He was, without doubt, the most peaceful and good-natured dog either Juliet or I could ever remember meeting. In fact, he was so well-mannered that months went by before we realised, much to our surprise, that neither of us had ever heard him bark. Just to be sure, we asked the girls, and they both confirmed that neither of them had heard even a tiny *woof* from Dexter. How could none of us have noticed that our beautiful boy was a silent partner in our family?

There was certainly nothing wrong with him. We'd had him health-checked at the vets when he was having is vaccinations. He certainly wasn't deaf, and he made lots of contented little snuffling noises while he was sleeping, so he was fully capable of vocalising, so we had to assume he was so happy and contented that he just hadn't felt the need to bark yet.

Meanwhile, life continued as normal, the dogs were all happy and contented, the girls returned to school after the summer holidays, and Juliet was doing quite nicely with her recently formed mobile dog-grooming business. She'd built up a small but regular following and customers were being added week by week. I was working on my latest novel and things were going well, until, one day, after returning home from a grooming job, Juliet complained of a severe pain in her right wrist.

Now, I have to say that Juliet almost never complains if she has a slight pain, or a headache for example. So, for her to complain of *severe pain*, I knew it had to be serious.

"Did you hurt it or perhaps pull a muscle or your tendons while you were on that last job?" I asked, trying to think of how she'd injured herself.

"No, but it did start to ache about halfway through the clipping," she replied.

She swallowed a couple of paracetamol tablets, washed down with a drink of water I passed to her, and I made dinner that evening, and encouraged her to rest her hand and arm as much as possible. The following day, the pain hadn't subsided and in fact, had grown worse. Whether she liked it or not, Juliet was going to have to pay a visit to the doctor. There was no way she could carry on grooming dogs if doing so was going to cause her such pain.

We made her an appointment for the next day and after seeing the doctor, a crestfallen Juliet announced that the diagnosis was that she was suffering from carpal tunnel syndrome. This was something I'd heard of and I once knew someone, a friend who had the same problem. I could recall his wrist and fingers being held in a form of wire 'cage' for weeks until he gained full use of his hand again.

Juliet was adamant she wasn't going to have the operation. She couldn't afford to be out of commission for two or more months. Apart from her grooming business, she had a house to run, two girls to look after, not to mention our twelve dogs, who still had to be walked twice a day and generally cared for. She decided she'd take the painkillers the doctor prescribed and see if the pain eased off, and then try and go back to work. Alas, it wasn't to be, as, the first time she went to do a grooming job a few weeks later, she came home in a lot of pain. She was extremely upset, when we jointly agreed she would have to give up her fledgling dog grooming business, which had really looked like it was going to be a great success. Some of her customers even begged her to carry on, but she had to explain that her health had to come first, and they reluctantly were forced to agree with her. From that day forward, she has restricted herself to grooming our own dogs, and as they require little in the way of clipping, (only Dylan, Penny and Cassie have long fur), and don't need doing too often, she can cope with that minimal amount of work, though she still suffers for a day or two after a grooming session.

Juliet is nothing if not resilient and she decided to find an alternative to her grooming business. It didn't take her long to find one. A friend happened to ask her one day, if she knew of any dog walkers, as she needed one for a few hours each week. Juliet had what I call her 'lightbulb moment' and instantly replied, "As a matter of fact, I do know of one...me!"

Needless to say, she got the job and over the next few months built up a clientele of dog owners who were prepared to pay for their dogs to be walked, while they were out at work or for some other reason. Some of them have been with her for years now, and those dogs would certainly miss her if she were ever to give up dog walking. I'm sure that in addition to walking our dogs, if you add the miles she must cover walking other people's dogs, Juliet must walk between fifteen and twenty miles a week. No wonder she's so trim and fit!

But, back to the star of our story. As the months passed, it became obvious to us all that Dexter, (or Mr. D), as we affectionately called him, wasn't what you'd call an overly energetic dog. He was more aristocratic than your average dog. While the others felt a sense of visceral exhilaration when they were loosed from their leads, and loved nothing better than running around, playing with their tennis balls or other toys, or just generally having fun play-fighting or interacting with us and so on, Dexter preferred a slow canter around the perimeter of the action, a little like a general surveying his troops. If there were bushes or trees close by, he loved nothing more than delving into or under them, exploring to see what treasures he might unearth.

With his royal blue collar standing out against his sleek, black coat, and his white chest leading the way, he really was a good-looking dog and he attracted many comments from people we met while on our walks. Dexter loved the smaller playing field where I took my dogs, and he found great pleasure in foraging around in the shrubs and bushes that bordered the field. He'd happily lose himself in amongst them while Victoria, who always came on the afternoon walk, after finishing school for the day, the other dogs and I had fun on the field.

We were frequently joined by my friend, Maureen and her little Yorkshire Terrier, Cindy, and we'd often take Barney, who belonged to Trevor, an elderly neighbour of ours. While Tilly, Molly, even long-legged Sophie ran and played with their tennis balls, Dexter enjoyed himself in his own way, exploring every nook and cranny of the undergrowth. One day, Victoria decided to try and train him to play 'fetch' and she followed him to the bushes, where she found a piece of a broken branch from one of the bushes. It was about a foot long, and she decided it would make a passable stick. Over the next ten minutes she patiently attempted to interest Dexter in the stick, without much success. Then, she had an idea. She clipped Dexter's lead onto his collar, then, she threw the stick as far as she could. She started running, not too fast, and Dexter had no choice but to run with her until they reached the stick. She picked it up and without waiting, threw it again, running with Dexter once again. After doing this about five times, she unclipped Dexter's lead and threw the stick, shouting, "Come on Dexter," as she set off in the direction of the stick. Much to my surprise, Dexter set off with her, ran beside her and when he reached the stick, he picked it up, walked a few paces to where Victoria now stood and dropped it at her feet.

"Good boy, Dexter," she gleefully exclaimed, having got Dexter to do something so unexpected. In an effort to keep him interested in this new game, she promptly threw the stick again, and this time Dexter took off on his own, picked up the stick and proceeded to walk around with it in his mouth, looking very pleased with himself. Over the next few days, she worked hard, trying to train Dexter to run and fetch the stick, but it was rather a hit and miss affair. Sometimes he'd show a little enthusiasm for the game and at other times he'd ignore it completely, and just disappear into the bushes for a quiet period of exploration of the undergrowth. Still, that was just his way, and there was no way we could be angry with him. Dexter was just... being Dexter!

Dexter on the playing field with Victoria and Barney

At last, one day, something happened that really seemed to bring Dexter to life, he found a friend, or rather, two to be precise. We were on the playing field one sunny, warm afternoon, when, on the far side of the field, we saw two young women entering the field through the large green painted, iron gates. They had two dogs with them, which, from a distance, looked like a pair of collies. They drew closer and I could see that I'd been correct. Both dogs were unrestrained by leads and were happily running free, chasing each other across the field. Tilly ran to meet them and the three of them were soon chasing each other in a game of 'tag,' doggie-style.

As the two young women neared us, they smiled and introduced themselves as Helen and Jenny, and the dogs as Rex and Meg. Rex was the larger of the two, very playful, and yet it was easy to see he was very subservient towards Tilly, who was obviously in charge of their game. Quite incredibly, they began racing around the playing field, with Tilly surprisingly leaving the collie in her wake. Helen and Jenny were astounded. They'd always thought Rex to be as fast as lightning.

"He is," I said, "but Tilly's faster than lightning."

They laughed and Helen said, "That's taught Rex he's not the fastest dog on the planet."

Meanwhile, we'd barely noticed that Dexter had slowly sauntered across to join us and was very intently making friends with Meg. How nice it was to see him actually interacting with another dog at last. The two of them were getting on like a house on fire, and when they actually wandered off into the bushes together, it was so touching to see them walking along together like a courting couple, with their tails wagging in unison. I told Helen not to worry, as Dexter was neutered and she laughed, apparently so was Meg, so we were safe from any unexpected puppies.

Tilly and Rex were completing their third lap of the field which meant they'd run about two and a half miles, and their tongues were lolling out of their mouths as they reluctantly decided to call it a day. Meanwhile we were all amused by the fact that Dexter and Meg were now involved in a game of synchronised roly-poly. They rolled to the right, and then to the left, in perfect unison.

"I think Dexter's in love," I laughed.

"I've never seen Meg like this before, have you?" Helen asked her sister.

"Never," Jenny replied. "Like you said, it must be love," she said to me, grinning all over her face.

Rex walked across and tried to get Meg's attention, but she only had eyes for Dexter. If ever there was a doggie romance, this was it. From that day, whenever we saw the sisters with Rex and Meg, the dogs followed the same routine, with Tilly and Rex sprinting like a pair of demons with the hounds of hell at their rears, around the field, and Dexter and Meg engaging in their strange but touching doggie romance.

It was such a shame when, a couple of years later, Helen came on to the field with Rex and told us that Meg had sadly died the previous day. They hadn't known she had cancer and by the time they found out it was too late for the vet to do anything about it. Dexter spent ages looking around the field, searching for his lost love, but of course, he never found her. He seemed quite depressed for weeks afterwards, but eventually, he appeared to get over the loss of his friend, but it was sad to see him moping about, searching for her whenever we went on the field. Who knows what goes through a dog's mind? We can't understand their feelings, but should at least understand that they possess them.

Helen and Jenny still brought Rex on the field and he continued his races with Tilly until they moved away after another year or so, and Tilly was left with nobody to race against. Did she miss him the way Dexter missed Meg? If she did, she didn't show it. Perhaps Tilly was more resilient than Dexter when it came to her sense of loss. We'll never know.

Looking for his friend

7

AMBASSADOR DEXTER

WITH SUCH A LARGE family of dogs, time seems to fly by, and before we knew it Dexter had celebrated his third year in our home. There's always something new going on and the dogs provide us with a constant source of entertainment and amusement. Sadly, as the years go by we are faced with the inevitable losses that dog owners all over the world have to go through. I'm not going to upset you with the tales of those we lost during the time Dexter was with us, but even one would have been too many. Juliet and I have had to learn to cope with the deep sense of loss that comes at such times and I do wonder if the other members of our canine family feel the same sense of grief and sadness when one of their family is no longer here.

I mention this only to explain why you are perhaps unfamiliar with the names of some of the dogs in this story. Each and every one of them was at one time a much-loved member of our family of rescue dogs, and every one of them is sadly missed. Sometimes, they were elderly when they came to us, and we didn't have the pleasure of loving them for as long as we would have wished, but they all have a place in our hearts, to this day. We never forget them.

Which leads me to mention two such dogs, no longer with us, but who shared in Dexter's life and enjoyed playing on the field at the time he was enjoying himself with Meg. They were Dinky and Misty, two little cross breed terriers who were real bundles of fun. Sometimes, I think they got on Dexter's nerves, they were so exuberant and full of fun. They would join us every day on the field and Victoria, in particular, had a great relationship with the pair of them. As young as she was, Victoria seemed to have a natural affinity for dog training and the dogs responded quite naturally to her as she set about training them to do all sorts of tricks, or just the basics of simple obedience training. It just appeared to come naturally to her.

Dinky and Misty adored Victoria and would do almost anything for her. She could get them to do things no-one else (including me) could manage. They'd run for her, jump for her, and run through little obstacle courses she'd set up for them.

Despite her tender years, Victoria certainly had a knack when it came to dog training. They seemed to respond to her quite naturally, her voice and her obvious love for them communicated itself to the dogs, who know when a human being is a 'doggie' person and respond accordingly. Though she's now grown up and no longer lives at home, the dogs still respond with excitement and joy when she comes to visit.

Dogs have an innate sixth sense and by some means we still don't understand, are able to sum a person up in seconds. How many people know of someone who tells a story of their dog meeting someone new for the first time, and begins growling at them as though giving their owner a warning about that person? Alternatively, some dogs will instantly take to a newcomer, making a big fuss of them and smothering them in doggie kisses. Victoria is one of the people who happens to fall into that category. When she was a little girl, her ambition was to be a police dog handler, and although that ambition never came to fruition, her dog handling skills remain intact.

Victoria with Misty and Dinky

DEXTER COULD NEVER DO the things Misty and Dinky did. He was content to do his own thing and one of the things we loved most about him was the fact that we never had to tell Dexter off for anything. Can you believe that? A dog who was never naughty or disobedient? It's true though, he really was, in that respect, a perfect dog. He absolutely loved his twice daily walks and lots of people in the village would often stop us to admire him. When they did, he'd do a perfect 'sit' and wouldn't budge until it was time to continue our walk. He'd lap up the attention, and loved the stroking and petting he'd receive from these perfect strangers, many of whom became friends over time, just because of our beautiful boy. He was like a sort of ambassador for our pack of dogs. People seemed to think they must all be like Mr. D. They weren't of course, but they wouldn't believe me when I told them so.

8

SNOOPY - DEXTER'S NEMESIS

I'VE PREVIOUSLY MENTIONED Dexter's sociability with other dogs. From the day we got him, we'd never had to worry about his reactions towards other dogs. That was, until the arrival of Snoopy! Juliet was looking at the local paper one afternoon, and came across an advert which stated *'Puppies for Sale.'* Having read it, she called me over to take a look, and I read, *'Puppies for sale, quarter Cavalier King Charles, only £20.'*

"Can we go and see them?" Juliet asked, before I'd even finished reading. I've always found it difficult to say 'no' to Juliet, especially when it comes to matters relating to dogs, and I thought it couldn't do any harm to just make a phone call and make enquiries about the puppies.

"Let's just phone up and see what they say about them first," I said.

Juliet was on the phone faster than a speeding express train. After a brief chat on the phone, during which she made a note of the lady owner's name, address and phone number, she said to me, "There were five pups originally, but there's only one left. The woman said, if she couldn't find a home for this one, she'd have to get rid of it. I didn't like the way she said it and I think she's likely to drown the poor thing if we don't take it."

"What's the address?" I asked and she passed me the sheet of paper she'd made notes on. One look at the address put me on what I can only call 'high alert'. Putting it politely, the address placed the puppy in what I'll call a not very nice area of town. It was a run-down area that was scheduled for demolition, with the residents earmarked for rehousing by the local council. I groaned inwardly. This was not the sort of place you'd want to leave your car unattended for more than ten minutes, but here we were, about to drive there and enter a house on one of the worst streets in town.

When we arrived, we were lucky to be able to park right outside the address we'd been given. The front garden was horribly overgrown and the paintwork on the front door was aged and peeling. I was almost afraid to knock, in case the door collapsed from shock. The woman who answered the door was friendly enough, though her appearance reflected that of the house.

She led us through to the kitchen, where the one solitary puppy lay wrapped in a scruffy grey blanket in a plastic dog bed that had definitely seen better days. My mind was already made up, and I could tell Juliet's was as well. There was no way we were going to leave the little puppy in that environment, especially when the woman repeated her comment about getting rid of the puppy if we didn't take him. Sensing strangers in the room, the puppy looked up and seeing us, jumped out of his bed and started jumping at us and wagging his tail, in typical fashion. If there was any Cavalier King Charles in his parentage, then I was born on the planet Venus! He was mostly white, with his most distinctive feature being the large black patch over one eye. He was a lovable little scamp, impossible not to love. Juliet picked him up, and was rewarded with non-stop puppy kisses.

"Has he had any of his vaccinations yet?" I asked the woman, who replied in the negative.

To be honest, I couldn't wait to get out of that house. To say it was dirty and scruffy would be an understatement. It was the sort of place where you wiped your shoes on the way out! I quickly withdrew a twenty-pound note from my back pocket, and said, "We'll take him."

Juliet looked relieved and we quickly gathered up the puppy and left the woman clutching her twenty-pound note as she saw us off at the door. We both let out sighs of relief at being away from that house and soon, we were home and intro-ducing the pup to our other dogs. They were all welcoming and friendly towards the newcomer, though Dexter seemed to keep out of his way as much as possible. Perhaps he wasn't keen on puppies.

The next thing Juliet did was whisk the as yet un-named puppy upstairs for a bath. He didn't smell very sweet, hardly surprising considering his previous lodgings. While he was in the bath, Juliet thought of a name for the new arrival, and shouted downstairs to me.

"I think Snoopy would suit him," she called to me.

"Hang on," I called back to her, and went upstairs to see how she was getting on with the bathing process. I guessed the little guy had never had a bath before in his short life and thought he might be finding it a traumatic experience.

Traumatic? He was loving it. There he was, covered in shampoo suds, and trying to romp around and play in the shallow water in the bath. As Juliet began to rinse him off under the shower, he did his best to catch the water jets, and managed to give Juliet a good soaking.

I couldn't help laughing, and as Juliet tried to dry herself, before drying the dog, I said, "I think Snoopy would be a great name for him, and anyway, after getting soaked like that, you deserve to pick his name."

So, it was officially decided, Snoopy it was!

After drying Snoopy off as much as possible with a towel, Juliet took him downstairs and let him out in the garden with the other dogs. He loved it, and was running around the back garden giving himself a do-it-yourself blow dry in the warm, fresh air. The other dogs were really interested in the new puppy and a couple of them immediately began running around with him and trying to play with him. He was tiny compared to them of course, so he got knocked down a few times, but he just got back up again and carried on the game.

Over the next few weeks Snoopy showed himself to be quite intelligent and was very easy to house train, and loved playing with the toys we bought him. He especially loved his rope tug toy and any kind of ball. Unfortunately, the tug toy led to an unfortunate and painful (for me) incident. Snoopy was following me through the hall one day, and I happened to have his tug toy in my hand, hanging down, within his reach. In playful exuberance, Snoopy jumped up and tried to grab his toy, but unfortunately, grabbed my leg instead. His very sharp teeth sank into the muscle at the back of my leg and the blood simply poured down my leg. I called Juliet who reacted quickly, wrapping a cold, wet towel round my leg in an attempt to stop the bleeding. Eventually, when the blood stopped leaking through the towel, she removed it and was shocked to see how deeply his little puppy teeth had penetrated, and I was shocked to feel how painful the leg was.

In the end, I had to visit my doctor's surgery, where I was examined by the doctor, and then passed over to one of the practice nurses, who applied some horrible looking yellow balm to the pad of a bandage which she then fastened to my leg. I was given a week's supply of dressings, with instructions to apply a fresh one each day, together with the yellow medicinal balm, for which I was given a prescription.

Poor Snoopy greeted me with excitement and much tail wagging on my return home, without any idea of the pain he'd accidentally caused me. It wasn't his fault of course, and the leg healed in about three or four weeks. Now, you know the old saying, *Lightning never strikes twice in the same place?* Well, in my case, it did, because about a month after my leg had recovered, I stupidly walked through the hall, tug toy in hand, and suddenly felt that familiar sharp, stabbing pain, as Snoopy's teeth, aiming for his toy, missed the target and again sunk into my leg!

Back to the surgery I went, blood seeping through the temporary bandage Juliet had applied. To say the nurse was amused was putting it lightly. She couldn't believe the same puppy had done the same thing to the same leg so soon after the leg had healed. Which he had, of course, in all innocence.

I left the surgery with more yellow stuff painted on my leg, more bandages and another prescription for the balm, which had, they told me, been specially formulated for the treatment of dog bites, to help prevent infection.

From that day, I made damned sure not to dangle Snoopy's tug toy from my hand if ever I had to carry it from one room to another. My leg remained safe from that day onwards.

Meanwhile, we went through the usual routine with having a new puppy, vaccinations, health check, microchipping etc, and once he was fully protected, Snoopy was cleared to join the gang on the village's two playing fields. He was a happy little soul, but even when he was with me and Victoria on the smaller playing field, we noticed Dexter always gave Snoopy something of a wide berth. We'd no idea why, but Dexter just hadn't taken to the puppy the way the other dogs had.

Perhaps Snoopy's favourite game was one I invented with him and an old partially deflated football we found on the field one day. He already loved playing with balls of all sizes, but I thought we might have some fun with this one. Getting his attention, I put the ball down at my feet, and began rocking from side to side. Snoopy caught on to the fact this was a new game, and then I said loudly, "Noopy...Noo!" the 'noo' bit I sort of stretched the word out and raised my voice so it came out like a command, and Snoopy took off after the ball, and then caught up to it, picked it up, and brought it back, dropping it at my feet for me to do it all over again. This remained Snoopy's favourite game throughout the years to come.

One day, we'd been out for a couple of hours on a Sunday afternoon, and when we returned, Juliet noticed a bottle of wine was missing from the wine rack in the kitchen. A quick look around the kitchen failed to locate the bottle, and I jokingly commented, "Maybe one of the dogs is a secret wine drinker."

After I said that, Juliet began to look through the dog beds, and I said, "I was only joking."

And yet, a minute later, she held up a bottle, which was hidden under a blanket in Snoopy's bed. I laughed and laughed, and Juliet joined in. The little rascal had somehow pulled the bottle down, out of the wine rack, dragged it (or rolled it), across the floor and then somehow manoeuvred it over the lip and into his bed, and then covered it with his blanket. Did he see it as a toy, or some kind of doggie treasure? That's something we'll never know as we quickly found a new home for the wine rack, out of the reach of doggie mouths or paws.

Snoopy with tug toy

One day, the rather fragile peace between Dexter and Snoopy was broken, when for reasons we're still not sure of, as Snoopy was walking past Dexter, who was lying in his bed, Dexter began growling, and then, totally unprovoked, he leapt up and chased Snoopy from the room. We were shocked, to say the least. This was the nearest we'd ever seen Dexter come to any kind of aggression. Admittedly, he made no attempt to attack Snoopy, but he'd definitely made it clear to Snoopy, not to encroach on his space.

After that day, we kept a close watch on the two of them, and Dexter would often growl, a low, throaty growl, as Snoopy walked past him. Snoopy just ignored him most of the time and took care to give Dexter a wide berth. The funny thing was, there was no problem between them when we went for walks together, only in the kitchen at home. Even in the lounge, they were perfectly peaceful together, so work that one out if you can, we never did.

Snoopy was with us for six years, despite his uneasy relationship with Dexter, until, we allowed him to go and live with an elderly neighbour of ours. Mavis had always loved him, and had recently lost her own little dog. Her granddaughter was a close friend of our Rebecca, who told us that Mavis was very lonely living on her own, and would it be possible for her to have Snoopy. She would love him and give him lots of walks and give him her total attention.

Juliet and I thought long and hard about it, and decided that, as he'd only be living round the corner from us, and as he'd get loads of love and fuss from Mavis, and we'd still see plenty of him, we'd give it a trial to see how he got on with her.

Mavis was over the moon with the arrangement and welcomed Snoopy with open arms, and gave him a lovely home, where he settled in with her in no time at all. We'd see her going past our house three or four times a day, walking Snoopy towards the large playing field, where she could confidently let him off his lead to play and run. Juliet would clip his claws whenever they needed doing and we all saw lots of him. Sometimes Mavis's granddaughter would take him for walks as well, so Snoopy certainly got plenty of exercise. Mavis was so happy to have him as a companion, and Snoopy seemed perfectly happy to be living with her, though whenever he saw us while out for a walk, he'd come to us for a love and a fuss, before happily going on his way. We were happy too, because we felt we'd done a good thing in making an old lady happy and because we'd given Snoopy a Dexter-free environment, (and vice-versa of course).

All went well, until one day, when we saw Mavis on her own, without Snoopy. She told us he'd been ill for a week or two, and when she'd taken him to the vet, they'd discovered he had a massive, cancerous tumour, and that sadly, it was inoperable. Poor Mavis had been faced with that terrible decision that comes to all dog owners sooner or later and because she didn't want her beloved Snoopy to be in pain or suffer the effects of the tumour, she allowed the vet to help him cross the Rainbow Bridge. Snoopy was gone, and we were all upset at his passing, and especially sad for Mavis, who had lost her faithful and constant companion. He was eleven years old when he went to the bridge, and they were eleven happy years for Snoopy, who was always loved throughout his life. Rest in Peace, little fella.

9

END OF THE CHICKEN

DEXTER'S STORY wouldn't be complete without mentioning his chicken. You might remember that before I collected Dexter form the Dog Pound, back in the beginning of this story, I mentioned the 'squeak-less' rubber chicken I bought for him at the same time as his large, hard plastic 'teething ring'. So far, I haven't made any reference to his chicken, so I'd better put that right.

As you've been reading Dexter's story (or should that be Dexter's Tale?), you might have realised that dog toys didn't play a big part in his life. Unlike the other dogs who would happily spend hours playing with, (and systematically destroying) all manner of dog toys, Dexter was happy with his big ring and, you've guessed it...his chicken.

No matter what the manufacturers claim about their often very expensive products, we've yet to come across a dog toy that can withstand the teeth and jaws of a pack of highly playful rescue dogs, which includes three Staffies and three Staffy crosses, (more about the crossbreeds later in the story). Some of the toys we've bought over the years have lasted no more than a couple of hours before being left in multiple pieces on the floor. Others have been lucky to last a day or two, but they invariably end up being massacred by the pack!

The only exceptions to escape this sad and sorry fate have been the two blue and white teddy bears we bought for Tilly and Dylan in their first weeks with us, Dexter's teething ring, and that chicken!

Dylan, Tilly and teddy bear!

How Dexter's chicken survived as long as it did is nothing short of a miracle. Most toys we bought for our dogs had a very short life span, some less than a day, most managing to last a week or two, before succumbing to the jaws and the teeth of our over-exuberant pack of playful pups. It reached a stage where we stopped buying 'official' dog toys and found other things for them to amuse themselves with, old bones, sticks, plastic bottles and so on. After all, they're dogs and don't know the difference between a shop-bought toy and a Lucozade bottle.

Dexter was an exception. His big teething ring lasted him for about three or four years, until one day, we found he'd finally bitten through it, and it was left with two sharp ends. It was finally consigned to the bin, much to Dexter's disgust. The look he gave me when I dropped it in the bin made me feel like a mass murderer. Sorry, Mr. D.

As for his chicken, the fact it survived so long is a testament to the way the rest of our dogs seemed to respect Dexter. I never, ever, saw any of them try to take hold of Dexter's chicken. I don't know if dogs have some secret way of communicating, but if they do, Dexter had obviously sent the word round the pack. Hands (or should I say Paws) off! It led a totally charmed life, and even when Dexter got hold of it and tossed it around, as he did in rare moments of exuberance, it never seemed to suffer any damage. We would most often see him with it in his bed, where he'd lie with it for ages, often sucking at it or gently chewing its splayed-out legs. I honestly don't remember exactly how the chicken met its demise, but seem to recall Juliet finding it one day with its head bitten off. I have absolutely no idea how (or who) was responsible for this terrible act of chicken destruction, but, like Dexter's ring, it found its final resting place in the rubbish bin.

Dexter and chicken

AFTER THE LOSS of his ring and his chicken we found it difficult to get Dexter interested in any other toys. Maybe he went
into a life-long sulk after losing his two treasured toys, I don't
know. I even went out and bought the nearest thing I could find
to his large teething ring, a new blue one, but he wouldn't touch
it. I tried to get him interested in it, Juliet tried, and the girls
tried, but he just rejected it and we ended up giving it to the
other dogs, who in turn had great fun with it. I felt sorry for
Dexter, but I couldn't force him to like something he didn't
want, could I?

Thankfully, Victoria had at least got him vaguely interested
in playing with a stick now and then on the playing field, so at
least he managed an occasional run around, even though it only
lasted a few minutes. Still, it wasn't as if Dexter was over-
weight. He always looked sleek and trim, was one of the fittest
dogs I'd ever known. Each year, when he went for his annual

booster vaccination, he underwent his health check-up and everything was fine, heart, lungs, liver function etc, and his weight remained constant, sometimes varying by no more than a kilogram or two from the previous year.

There was one area where he could be a bit possessive, and that was with bones. We had a friend who used to visit a traditional butcher in a nearby village and he used to be given a nice, large, juicy bone for his dog. One day, he arrived at our house with a whole bag full of those fresh bones, a present for our dogs. Of course, they loved them, a real tasty mixture, some ham, some beef and some lamb bones.

All was well until some of the dogs, having gnawed every last bit of taste from their own bones, decided to 'borrow' some of the bones belonging to other dogs. Now, most of our dogs were quite good at sharing bones, toys etc, but this was the time when we saw another side of Dexter's character. He did NOT take lightly to anyone else trying to muscle in on HIS bone. First, he growled, next he picked his bone up and walked away to another part of the garden or whichever room he happened to be in, and if that didn't work, Dexter actually SNAPPED at the prospective doggy thief! He didn't actually try to bite the other dog, but he was definitely making it known that nobody was allowed to touch or play with what he saw as his personal bone, which he was saying in doggie language, was his own private property, and certainly not for sharing.

As the nice, juicy, tasty bones were an obvious item of potential dispute amongst our normally happy pack, we asked our kind-hearted friend not to bring any more fresh bones for the dogs, and we instead gave them an occasional 'filled bone', you know, the ready cooked bones that come with a meaty filling, and which the dogs loved to chew on, and lick the insides out, until, you've guessed it! Dexter obviously worked on a dog's first and second rules of acquisition, namely, *if it's in my mouth, it's mine*, and secondly, *if it was in your mouth and you drop it, and I pick it up, it's mine.*

That was the end of the filled bones, and taught us that as peaceable and placid as he was 99% of the time, when it came to the subject of bones, Dexter was a naughty, possessive boy, and we returned to our usual dog treats as a means of giving the dogs a reward, or a special treat.

I did however, find a new toy that Dexter was happy to accept, a giant, nylon bone! Made from the same material as his original 'teething ring' it was even the same colour. He loved it and spent many happy hours playing with it, and as with his ring, he'd walk around the house with it in his mouth, as though challenging anyone to try and take it from him. Of course, no one ever did. Every one of the dogs knew how possessive Mr. D. was when it came to his special toys, and very soon, the big bone joined Dexter in bed at night, where he could keep it safe.

Dexter's big bone

10

FEATHERED FRIENDS

OVER THE YEARS, Dexter has been known by a few names, Mr. D., Dexter the Seal, and latterly and the one that best describes him, Bird-Dog. Have I mentioned Dexter the Seal in the story yet? I don't think I have. Allow me to explain. From the beginning, Dexter never once showed any reluctance to go for a walk, no matter what the weather. Whether it was sunny, warm, icy-cold, thick with snow or pouring with rain, it was all the same to Dexter. We'd bought him a lovely dog coat, quite an expensive one too, but he just hated to wear it.

It was walking in the rain that earned him the Seal name. One day, as he and I walked in to the house after a walk in quite heavy rain, Juliet, waiting with a large bath towel to dry him off, took one look at him, laughed and said, "Look at him. He looks like a seal," and he did!

His fur was kind of slicked down and had that lovely 'wet look' that seals have when they emerge from the sea. If you've seen enough nature or wildlife shows on the TV, or been lucky enough to see one in real-life, you'll know exactly what I mean. Dexter had the kind of fur that was almost water repellent, so drying off didn't take long, and he soon returned to normal Dexter mode, but from that day, whenever we were approaching the door on returning from a walk in the rain, I'd call out, "Here comes Dexter the Seal." The name really suited him. Well, at least we thought so.

More importantly, as the years passed, Dexter developed the habit, on a nice day, whether it was sunny or not, of disappearing to the bottom of the garden, where we'd see him sitting near the bird table that was situated there, and which was regularly visited by all sorts of birds. When I added a second, smaller table our garden became a real haven for the local bird population. We were regularly visited by sparrows, starlings, blackbirds, robins, greenfinches, and even doves and pigeons. Every morning I'd put out seed, mealworms, two or three slices of crumbed bread and we also kept two fat ball holders stocked up for them.

Dexter appeared to be fascinated, watching the various birds coming and going about their business, and thanks to us watching him, watching them, we developed a greater knowledge of the regular visitors to our garden. Some of the homes around us have large, tall trees in their gardens and by watching closely, I was able to work out that a family (or two) of collared doves had their nests in one tree that overlooks our garden. Another tree was home to a family of blackbirds and we were regularly treated to the blackbird's beautiful song. I was pleased, one day, to see a family group of song thrushes on our tables. Over the years, I've worked out that the same families must nest year after year in the same places, and whether by some form of communication, or just good luck, they and their offspring use our bird tables as a regular feeding station. I've become quite an amateur expert on bird habits and identification, thanks to Dexter's 'hobby'.

As for Dexter, it took us a while to realise that he was

71

almost infatuated with his bird-watching. I took to observing him while he was enjoying the company of his feathered-friends and very soon, I realised something else. The birds had accepted Dexter's presence as being perfectly normal and weren't at all intimidated by him being so close to them. We all know how nervous and jumpy birds are when a person, dog or cat approaches them, but they weren't a bit afraid of Dexter.

I jokingly commented one day, "Perhaps they think he's a giant blackbird," and Dexter was thus landed with yet another nickname. I rather liked thinking of him as our very own Giant Blackbird.

This was confirmed for sure, one summer's morning, when I was watching from the window of the utility room and suddenly realised what was happening at the bottom of the garden.

"Juliet, you must see this," I called, as Juliet was sitting eating her breakfast in the kitchen. She came and stood next to me, and we were both amazed to see Dexter, sitting in his usual place, surrounded by birds, pecking around on the ground as birds do, none of them taking any notice of the rather large black dog seated in their midst. It was truly something we never expected to see. We were even more surprised when Dexter started to move from a sitting position to lie on his tummy. Surely, we thought, they will all fly away in panic now. No, they didn't! They just carried on pecking around him on the ground, feeding from the bird tables and clinging to the fat ball feeders, enjoying their morning feed. If we hadn't witnessed it for ourselves, we'd never have believed it, and yet, it had happened and this odd bird behaviour would be repeated many, many times in the years to come.

Sentry duty

It was obvious to us that somehow, Dexter had developed a very special relationship with the local bird population, which was evidenced by the fact that when one of the other dogs approached within a few yards of the daily avian activity, there'd be a sudden mass exodus, with poor old Dexter left looking up at the bird tables, wondering where all his little birdie buddies had disappeared to. He needn't have worried, because as soon as the other dogs went back indoors, with a great flapping of wings, descending like a cloud, the birds would return.

The other important job that Dexter fulfilled while on his daily 'bird patrol' was as the birds' anti-cat protector. In the past, we'd notice the occasional cat sitting in the garden, and we'd send one or two of the dogs out to chase them off. Once Dexter was in place on 'sentry duty' we never saw a cat encroaching into our garden. He was now the birds' official bodyguard. We'll hear more about Dexter and the birds a little later.

11

DEXTER'S LUMPS

ABOUT THREE YEARS AGO, while grooming him, Juliet noticed that a lump had developed on Dexter's side. We were aware that some senior dogs can develop some lumps and bumps as they grow older, so initially we weren't too worried by it. Dexter didn't appear to be ill, and certainly wasn't bothered by the lump, especially when Juliet gave him his twice weekly hoovering.

That's right, Dexter loved being vacuumed all over, and while most of our other dogs ran a mile at the sight or sound of our Henry Vacuum cleaner, Dexter would trot up to Juliet and sit in front of her, waiting to be 'done'. Once he realised she was going to do him as well as the carpets, he'd stand up and let her vacuum his coat all over, loving every second of it. By the time she was finished, his coat positively gleamed! Strange dog, our Dexter.

On a serious note however, it was good that he didn't mind being vacuumed as, with all the time he spent with the birds, under the bird tables, his coat would often be covered in bird seed, and normal brushing wasn't always successful in ridding his coat of all of it. We jokingly half expected a few blades of grass to start sprouting up from his back. I think if he'd got his way, he'd have let Juliet go on hoovering his back for half an hour or more. It must have felt like an invigorating all-over body massage to him.

Returning to the matter of the lump, we kept a close watch on it, and gradually, over time both Juliet and I thought it was slowly getting larger. That's when we began to worry. Like all loving pet parents, we immediately thought the worst, that Dexter might have a tumour, perhaps cancer, all sorts of things went through our minds.

There's only one way to make sure," I said, "We'll have to get him checked out at the vets."

"And what if it's bad news?" Juliet replied with a worried look on her face.

"Let's be positive, and not think about that until there's something to worry about," I tried to reassure her.

Yes, you're right," she agreed with me. "It's probably just one of those lumps they sometimes get with old age."

The next day, I phoned and made an appointment for Dexter to see the vet. Luckily, they had an appointment free that evening, so after we'd fed all the dogs at tea time, Juliet helped me to load Dexter into the car, (with my disability, he was too heavy for me to lift by myself), and Dexter and I motored the three miles to the veterinary surgery. The girls at the surgery were surprised to see me as I walked in with Dexter. In all the years we'd had him, he'd never been ill, always the healthiest dog in the pack, and only ever went to the vet for his annual booster vaccination. The receptionists and a couple of the practice nurses all came to see him and all made a big fuss of him. Dexter positively lapped up the love and hugs he received from them all. Over the years, that's one thing I've loved about the people at my local Vets4Pets surgery. They really care about our dogs and always go out of their way to show them love and affection, and really put them at their ease, on what is normally a stressful experience for many dogs.

When Dexter's name was called, we walked into the consulting room, after stopping to have him weighed on the large scales that stood close to the consulting room doors. I can remember still, Dexter calmly walking onto the scales and sitting perfectly still until the vet had recorded his weight. I think, on that day, he was about 21 kilograms, around his normal weight, so no significant weight loss or gain since the last time he'd been.

The vet carried out an examination, and checked Dexter thoroughly. His heart, lungs and all vital organs were normal and he didn't have a temperature so she took the decision to take a biopsy of Dexter's lump, which I'd need to return for the following day.

The next day, I checked Dexter in first thing in the morning, as he'd have to have an anaesthetic before they carried out the procedure. I arranged to collect him that evening and left him in the care of the vet and staff.

Poor Dexter! In all the years we'd had him we'd never had to leave him at the vets before. He looked bereft as I walked out of the consulting room, leaving him with Helen, the veterinary nurse.

"Don't worry, Mr. Porter," she reassured me. "We'll take good care of him."

"I know you, will," I replied, feeling like a mass murderer as I left him staring after me. I know it was only a biopsy, but Dexter didn't know that, or that it was something to help him. All he knew was that he'd been abandoned at the vet, and he had no idea whether he'd ever see me again. Some people don't think of things like that when they leave their dogs at the veterinary surgery. Some dogs must feel even worse than Dexter obviously did, especially if they've been abandoned by a previous owner.

At home, the day passed normally, and soon enough the clock showed it was 5 pm, time for me to go and collect Mr. D. I called ahead to make sure he was ready for collection and was told I could come and get him whenever I wanted. I was in the car, and on the road in the blink of an eye, and within ten minutes, arrived at the surgery. When they brought him through to the consulting room, I swear I could see relief, happiness and unbridled joy on his face as soon as he saw me. I'd never seen his tail wag quite so fast, if that says anything. Helen, the nurse, informed me that he'd been a perfect patient, (what else, this is Dexter after all), and asked me to make an appointment for five days' time, by which time they should have the results of the biopsy from the lab. She also told me that while Dexter was under the anaesthetic, the vet had found a second lump, and had taken a sample from that one also. Looking at Dexter's side, I now saw the results of his time under the anaesthetic. He had two bare patches where they'd shaved his fur to get at the lumps, which were now clearly visible. The larger one, which was the one we'd found was quite a substantial growth, and the smaller one, while nowhere near as big, was still clearly and easily visible. Helen urged me not to worry too much and so, before leaving the surgery, I stopped off at reception and made Dexter's follow-up appointment.

Dexter was certainly pleased to be home and he was greeted in turn by all the dogs, who'd obviously been missing him during his day-long absence. One really nice thing about Dexter was that, unlike most of the dogs, he never rushed his food, usually taking his time, as though savouring every mouthful, but this time, he literally 'wolfed' his tea down as if he'd been starved for a week. Of course, he'd had no breakfast that morning, as he'd been starved prior to having the anaesthetic for the biopsy, so that explained his voracious appetite. To be honest, we hadn't expected him to be hungry when he came home, as usually, after undergoing any procedure that involved being anaesthetised, our dogs would still be slightly groggy when they came home, and weren't interested in food until the following day, but this was Dexter, and of course, he had to be different.

After having been welcomed home by humans and dogs alike, and with his tummy full, as soon as we opened the back door to let the dogs out, Mr. D. made a bee-line for the bird tables, as if he wanted to announce his return to his birdie friends. Of course, by that time in the evening there weren't many of his feathered friends around, but there were a few sparrows and starlings hopping about the place, and perching on the garden fence, the main bird table being occupied by a couple of young doves.

"I can fit on this pouffe, honestly"

Dexter had a good look around as if he was surveying his territory, and he looked up to watch the doves for a minute until he satisfied himself that all was well, in the land of Dexter's birds. In fact, that was the day I coined the phrase *Dexter's Birdland* to describe the bottom of our back garden. I thought perhaps this was his way of announcing to his feathered friends, *I'm back!*

He must have spent almost half an hour there, happily communing with nature, I thought, and then, the residual effects of the anaesthetic must have caught up with our boy, because he turned and left the birds in peace, slowly wandered back into the house, had a very big drink of water, and then plonked himself down in his bed, where he quickly fell asleep. He was soon snoring happily, (dreaming of his birdie pals, perhaps?), and in fact, Dexter slept from then right through till the following morning without even getting up to go out to answer nature's call at bedtime.

FIVE DAYS LATER, Dexter and I returned to the vets, where we were given the anxiously awaited results of the biopsy. The news was good. Both lumps were benign growths and ordinarily the vet wouldn't recommend removing them, but, owing to the position of the larger one, and the fact that those things, though benign, could go on growing, the vet in this case recommended that we have the larger one removed as if it did go on growing it could actually begin to put pressure on the lung, to which it was very close already. If we decided to go ahead and have it removed, he said we might as well remove the smaller one at the same time to make sure there was no chance of that one growing too, and affecting any of Dexter's internal organs.

I phoned Juliet from the surgery, and explained the situation and the vet's recommendation. I wanted to be sure we were both in agreement before authorising surgery for Dexter. She quickly agreed that it would be the best thing to do for Mr. D. and so I made an appointment for the following day. The sooner it was done, the sooner Dexter could get on with enjoying life.

Once again, we went through the usual pre-op procedure, nothing to eat after 8 pm, and nothing to drink after 7 am on the day of the operation. Poor Dexter was going through it a bit at this time and I felt really sorry for him, but comforted myself with the thought that it was all for the sake of his long-term well-being.

Just after 8 am, Juliet as usual helped me load Dexter in the car, and we set off for the surgery. Dexter clearly wasn't happy when I parked the car, got him out, and he saw we were heading for the front doors to the vet's surgery. He actually pulled back and tried to 'dig his paws in' to prevent us from going through the door and I had to drag my poor boy into the surgery. The staff saw me coming and the receptionist quickly came out from behind the counter to pet Dexter and reassure him. He perked up a bit at that, and again when one of the nurses arrived and also made a big fuss of him. By the time we were called into the consulting room, he'd calmed down considerably. Once there, I signed the necessary consent form for him to have the operation and the nurse promised to call me when he'd come round after the anaesthetic had worn off. Once again, I felt like a mass murderer, having to walk away and leave him with the nurse holding his lead, and his big eyes looking imploringly at me as if to say, "Don't leave me Dad!"

I gave him a big hug, and told him, "Don't worry Mr. D., I'll be back later."

Silly, I know, but I hoped that the tone of my voice would reassure him. Juliet and I spent the day doing all the normal things we usually did, but both of us were worried about Dexter. It may have been routine stuff for the vet, but every dog owner will know that you can't help worrying when your dog is going under anaesthetic and being operated on.

Sure enough, the nurse called as promised, soon after 2 pm that afternoon.

"Dexter's fine, Mr. Porter. The operation went smoothly, both lumps removed and he's just woken up. He's still a bit groggy, obviously, but he'll be ready for you to collect any time after 5 o'clock. Is it okay if we give him something to eat if he's hungry in a while?"

"Thank you," I replied, with relief in my voice. "I'm so happy he's okay. Yes, of course he can have something to eat if he's hungry. I'll be there at around quarter past five, if that's okay."

"That's fine," she replied. "I'll book you in for a 5.15 collection, so we can have him ready when you get here."

"That's great. Thanks, see you soon," I said, feeling happier than I'd felt all day.

Juliet shared my relief at the news and we both felt so much better as we embarked on our round of afternoon dog walks. After feeding all the dogs, at 4.30 I was anxious to get going and collect Dexter, so I set off a little earlier than planned in the hope I could pick him up a bit sooner. That proved to be no problem at the vets but when Dexter was brought in to the consulting room, he looked very sad and sorry for himself. He was obviously feeling sore after his operation.

The vet said, "Dexter's fine Mr. Porter. It'll take a little while for the effects of the anaesthetic to fully wear off and he'll be a bit sore at first. I've given him a painkilling injection and he should feel a lot better by tomorrow."

He gave me a large bottle of Metacam, anti-inflammatory painkiller which I was to give Dexter, once a day, from the next day, and also take him back to the vet for a post-op check in three days. I arranged that appointment straight away and then led a rather drunk-looking Dexter out to the car. One of the nurses came out with me to help me manhandle Dexter into the car, and I was soon heading for home. When I pulled up outside our house and opened the tailgate, Dexter was fast asleep, curled up in a tight ball on the comfy dog mattress in the back of the car. I left him there while I went in the house, and got Juliet to come out and help me to bring Dexter in.

Together, we gently woke our sleeping beauty, and carefully lowered him to the ground. Dexter looked really worn out and it took him a full minute, on rather shaky legs, to get from the car to the back door of the house, a distance of no more than ten yards. The other dogs, as usual, tried to greet him, but all he was interested in was climbing into his bed. Once there he swiftly fell back into a deep sleep and certainly wasn't interested in food or anything else. He did wake up a couple of hours later, by which time Juliet and I were seated at the kitchen table, chatting together, and to our surprise he sort of clambered up, paws on the table, to say hello.

"Hi mate," I said. "Feeling better now?"

"I bet he wants to go to the toilet," the ever-practical Juliet said, and of course, she was right.

As soon as I went to the back door and opened it, Dexter slowly made his way down the garden, stopping for a pee on the way, and then, unbelievably, went to check out the bird tables. By now, it was late evening and all the birds had gone for the day, having returned to their nests or night-time perches, but despite having undergone surgery just a few hours previously, good old Dexter wanted to make sure everything was okay in his own little bird sanctuary.

Just woken up, saying hello

Dexter slept well that night, as you'd have expected, and the following day, he was much brighter in himself, and even wanted to go for his morning walk, but of course, he couldn't. There were to be no walks at all for the first three days after his operation and only short walks on his lead for a couple of weeks after that.

Dexter was certainly a fast healer, and right from the start, he gave no indication that he might be in any pain or discomfort. When he went for his first post-op check-up, the vet was delighted with him, and commented on how quickly the operation wounds were closing. Normally, he'd want the stitches to stay in for two weeks, but if Dexter continued as he was currently doing, he'd be happy to take them out in a week, meaning he'd have had the stitches for just ten days. We made his next post-op appointment for a week from that day, and sure enough, the vet was happy to remove the stitches at that point.

Checking his territory, Dexter's Birdland

He said that, as long as there was no running and jumping around, Mr. D. could resume his normal walking routine, including off-lead sessions of about ten minutes at a time. As this was 'Mr. Laid Back Dexter' we had no worries on any of those points. Now, all he needed to do was to grow back the fur to cover the bare patches on his side. They looked like a couple of hatches that had been cut into his side, poor fella.

It took a few months for his fur to grow back and fully cover the operation scars, but eventually, a fully-furred Dexter took the place of the patched-up version. We were treated to a lovely warm and sunny spell during his recovery period, and when he wasn't spending time with his birdie friends at the bottom of the garden, Dexter liked to do a spot of sunbathing. With him and little Muffin being black, their coats tended to attract the heat of the sun, and yet, while the other dogs had the sense to come in to the house to cool down when it got too hot, those two would lie out there until they were virtually cooking and we'd have to make them come indoors to be cooled down. We have a large floor-standing kitchen fan and they would lie on the wooden parquet kitchen floor, right in front of it, until they were comfortably cool again.

As summer wore on, everyone was happy. Normal Dexter service had been fully resumed!

"Am I done yet?"

12

DEXTER THE INCREDIBLE BIRD-DOG

YOU MAY REMEMBER EARLIER in the book, I promised to tell you more about Dexter and his birds later. Well this is the 'later' I was referring to.

It was the summer of 2017, which was a particularly good summer where we live, and Dexter and all the dogs were doing well, health-wise, except for Sasha, who many of you will know, suffers from the terrible blight of canine epilepsy. You may even have read her story in the first book of this series, titled simply, *Sasha, A very special dog tale of a very special epi-dog*. She'd been stable for a long time, but over the summer months, she began to have regular seizures again. She began having seizures, on average, every month, sometimes just the one, and sometimes a cluster-fit of two of three seizures, almost one after the other.

So, I spent a lot of time going backwards and forwards to the vet, and Sasha, as always, met it all head-on with a wagging tail and a big Staffy smile on her face. In between vet visits and my writing, (I was busy writing *A Very Mersey Murder* at the time), I also had to contend with some personal health issues, which made walking more painful for me than it had ever been. It took about four or five months to stabilise Sasha again, but she never lost her sense of fun and playfulness, especially with the puppy Honey.

Sasha and Dexter

So anything that could bring a smile to my face would be a welcome distraction. Now, I'm sure a lot of you will have seen those wonderful TV shows, by Sir David Attenborough and other great wildlife film producers, showing all manner of real-life situations featuring the big cats, lions, tigers etc. Have you ever seen the ones that show a lion or a tiger relaxing in the heat of the day, with surprisingly, small birds perched on their backs?

If we ever needed confirmation that the relationship between Dexter and the birds was something special, this was it. As he lay on his tummy on the special mat we'd provided for him for a little comfort close to the bird tables, we had to blink twice, and rub our eyes to make sure we weren't seeing things, because there was not one, not two, but THREE sparrows perched on Dexter's back! I tried to get a photo of this amazing sight through the utility room window, but it was too far away, and even on maximum zoom you couldn't really make out the sparrows clearly, but please take my word for it, they were there.

Dexter looked perfectly at peace with the three little birds on his back, and I tried to get closer for another photo opportunity, but as I crept out of the back door and took two paces towards them, they must have seen or sensed me, and they flew away. But now we knew that our beautiful 'bird dog' Dexter, was really something special. Over time we witnessed further examples of this happening, usually with sparrows but on one occasion at least I saw a pair of fledgling starlings happily perched on his back. (Uncle Dexter, eh?)

One last sunbathe, Muttley as always, by his side

As I just mentioned, we had provided Dexter with a special mat for him to lie on when he was on 'bird duty' and if any other dog tried to lie on it when Dexter wasn't around, I could swear that there'd be a sudden chattering amongst the birds from the trees around us, as if they were calling him to tell him his place had been stolen, and sure enough he'd come sauntering out of the back door, lope down the garden and the offending dog would look up, see him coming, and quickly vacate Dexter's mat, and he'd recommence his bird watching.

We didn't really notice at the time, but with hindsight both Juliet and I agree that it was around this time that Dexter seemed to slow down a lot in terms of his general activity level, Whether it was the onset of old age, (he was ten by now), the beginnings of an illness, or just general laziness, we'll never know. Dexter of course, was never a particularly energetic dog, so a bit of laziness mixed with his love for the birds and his desire to be near them as much as possible, is probably the nearest to the truth.

I mentioned the puppy Honey a few paragraphs ago, and her playing with Sasha. I think little Honey deserves a brief mention here. At the time, Victoria was living at home and working, (yes, working, doesn't time fly?) in the offices of an insurance company. One day, she arrived home one evening and asked her Mum to go outside for a minute, as there was something she wanted to show her. The 'something' was an eight week old puppy, that Victoria had named Honey, due to her honey coloured fur, and that Victoria said was her Christmas present to her Mum. We were initially angry with Victoria, as we'd made it quite clear for some time that we didn't want any more dogs. Both Juliet and I are not getting any younger and looking after ten dogs, (eleven with the addition of Honey), is virtually a full-time job for both of us, and at the end of each day, we literally collapse into bed, exhausted. We're up at 5.30 am every day to begin the daily process of caring for our beloved dogs, starting with letting them out, then it's breakfast for them all, then by the time Juliet and I have bathed, washed, shaved, (me, not Juliet) and whatever, it's time to begin dog walking, which we do in shifts between us. I should mention again, that Juliet, in addition to walking our dogs, is also a dog walker and so walks miles every day, so you can see why she's tired in an evening.

Anyway, we couldn't be angry for long, as who can be angry with a tiny puppy in the house? Right from day one, Sasha took over as a surrogate mum for the puppy. She'd done the same when we adopted the three puppies, Petal, Muffin and Digby, seven years ago. She's a natural mother is Sasha. She assumed the role of caring for the little dog, teaching her how to be a part of the pack and perhaps, most importantly, how to play! Even now, with Honey fully grown, Sasha happily spends hours playing with her. Doing zoomies around the kitchen furniture is one of their favourite games, and the noise they make when one of them bangs into a kitchen cupboard door rattles the room. That's the point where I banish the pair of them to the garden and off they go, the zoomies simply transferred to the larger space, where they can have much more fun. If they get fed up with the zoomies they start play fighting, and I swear that a stranger, anyone who didn't know them, would think their play fights were for real. They make some awful noises and to see Honey gnawing on Sasha's leg, as if it's a bone, is hilarious. Sasha lets Honey get away with almost anything until she decides 'enough is enough' and asserts herself and forces a sulking Honey to cease the game and rest.

'Mummy' Sasha with Honey

I've mentioned Honey to demonstrate once again Dexter's wonderful, placid nature. Welcoming a bouncy, playful, noisy young puppy to the home is never easy for an older dog and Dexter could have been forgiven if he'd given the young upstart a hard time when he was suddenly faced with the young whippersnapper. But no, Dexter welcomed the little pup into the home with hardly the blink of an eye. Even when Honey jumped all over him while he was asleep or just resting in his bed, Dexter just shrugged it off and never once showed any sign of aggression or irritation with the new pack member. A perfect gent, our Dexter.

It seemed that, as long as he had his two daily walks and had plenty of time to spend with his birdie friends and was well-fed, Dexter the bird-dog couldn't have been happier. What we didn't know at the time though, was that there was a great big cloud on the horizon which would impact greatly on Dexter, and on all our lives.

Happy Dexter

13

THE LAST YEAR, THE LAST DAY

EARLY IN 2018, Dexter developed a cough. We didn't think it was anything serious. We'd had lots of dogs who suffered from a cough now and then and now as we usually did, we treated it with Children's Benylin cough medicine, which a vet had recommended to us years ago. At first it seemed to be doing the trick, but the improvement we saw in him proved to be only temporary.

Feeling sorry for our boy, I made an appointment at the vet for him. Arriving a little early for our 5.15 appointment, we were welcomed by the girls on reception. With ten dogs, I tend to be quite a frequent visitor to the surgery and am on friendly terms with all the vets and staff. In the few minutes before we were seen, the girls all came out to see Dexter. Apart from the previous year's booster jab, they hadn't seen him since he'd had his lumps removed a couple of years ago, so everyone wanted to fuss him and cuddle him and, of course, ask me why we were there this time.

A few minutes later, we were called in to see the vet. Dexter's vet at this time was Ximo Huertas Montón. Ximo, (pronounced Cheemo) is Spanish, and speaks excellent English, so no communication problem there, as I know can sometimes happen when dealing with a vet for whom English is not their first language.

Most recently he had developed a very special relationship with Sasha, following a really nasty series of seizures, after which she had to be taken in to the vets, where she was kept for a day, for treatment, which included being on a drip for a few hours to get fluids in to her, and various tests. Ximo fell in love with Sasha, (who doesn't?), and when I called to collect her in the evening, he walked out from the treatment area, carrying Sasha in his arms, like a baby. She was perfectly capable of walking, but Ximo wanted to give her some extra cuddles before we went home.

I said to Sasha, "Shall we go home now, Sasha?" at which point Ximo took a seat in the waiting room, still holding Sasha in his arms. He was totally enamoured with her, and eventually he rose, but instead of putting her down so she could walk to the car, he insisted on carrying her to the car for me, and once there, he gently placed her on the dog mattress in the back of the car, and gave her one last cuddle before I closed the tailgate. You don't get service and affection like that from all vets. Ximo is truly an amazing and very compassionate man.

Now, he was about to play a massive part in Dexter's life. It took less than a minute for him to develop a rapport with Mr. D., who took to Ximo immediately. He examined our boy, thoroughly, getting down on the floor with him, rather than lifting him up to the examination table, which put Dexter even more at ease. He was so thorough that I began to suspect that this was not a case of a simple cough, as I'd thought.

Ximo talked to Dexter all the time, making a lifelong friend as he did so. Finally, he stood and faced me.

"Brian," he said, "I'd like to keep Dexter for a few hours to do some tests. I can hear some crackling in there, and he may have some fluid on his lungs but it's best to check it out before I prescribe any medication for him."

"Okay, Ximo. If you think that's best, I'm okay with it."

"The tests are totally non-evasive, so he won't need sedation," Ximo told me, and I gave Dexter a cuddle before leaving him. This time, he didn't seem to mind me deserting him. Obviously, Ximo's words, tone of voice and physical contact with him had won Dexter's trust and I was soon outside the surgery, from where I called Juliet on my mobile phone to let her know what was happening.

"Oh heck," she said when I told her Ximo was keeping Dexter in for tests. "It's not just a cough then?"

"Apparently not. He might have fluid on his lungs but we won't know until he's had the full examination and the tests."

We spent a worrisome day, as we waited for the time to pass, until at last I could go and collect Dexter. As always, Ximo greeted me with a smile and a handshake, something that's always impressed me about him, and invited me into a consultation room. He didn't have Dexter with him and for a minute, I was worried, but he immediately put my mind at rest.

"Don't worry, Dexter's fine. I'll bring him through in a minute. He's just having some snacks with the girls out back."

Vet and patient

Dexter had obviously made himself at home in the surgery, much as Sasha does whenever she visits. Sasha always has to go out the back and say hello to all her friends at the practice!

While we waited for Dexter to finish his snacks, Ximo gave me the results of Dexter's tests and x-rays.

"Unfortunately, Brian, Dexter has a build-up of fluid on his lungs, and he also has a problem with his heart, which is beating with an unnatural rhythm. I'm going to put him on medication to try to clear his lungs and to regulate his heart beat."

For a minute, I didn't know what to say. I was filled with a sense of guilt at not seeking veterinary help sooner.

"Ximo, we thought it was just a cough and that you'd give him some meds and it would clear up in a week or two."

Ximo seemed to sense my feelings and quickly sought to reassure me,

"It's not your fault," he said. "This has probably been going on for a while without any symptoms showing up. The first symptom you noticed was the cough, and you tried to treat it, and when it didn't clear up, you brought him in. You've done your best for him, really."

"Thanks for the reassurance," I felt a little better. "What's the prognosis for Dex?"

"First of all, I have to tell you, he isn't ill, as such. These are really the symptoms of the onset of old age. We can do our best to treat Dexter with medication, but he's not going to make a full recovery and be a young dog again."

"I understand," I replied.

"I'll go and fetch him now, and his tablets for you to give him."

He left the room and returned a couple of minutes later with Mr. D.

"Hi Dex," I said when he walked into the room. "Time to go home, mate."

Dexter's tail wagged with happiness at seeing me there to collect him. I thanked Ximo, who asked me to take Dexter back in a month so he could check on his progress. Then we made a quick stop at reception to fill in Dexter's insurance claim form, and in no time at all, we were outside, walking to the car. Unlocking the car, I lifted the tailgate and to my amazement, Dexter leaped up and into the back, where he promptly plonked himself down on the dog mattress in the back, curled up, and went to sleep before we'd even moved off. It had been a long, stressful day for our Mr. D.

Back home, I explained everything to Juliet, who like me, asked the same soul-searching question.

"Could we have done anything sooner?" she asked.

"No, don't think like that. Ximo said it's just old age, and taking him sooner wouldn't have made much of a difference."

We both gave Dexter lots of extra love that evening, because the thought of him getting old and not being able to do much to help him, left us both feeling quite impotent to do anything positive for him. Once we started him on his tablets, he seemed to pick up a little and his cough, though it didn't go away, became less rasping and not so loud. Perhaps the meds were helping him, a bit anyway.

When I took him back after a month, Ximo examined him fully once again. When he listened to his lungs, he was happy to be able to tell me that there was less 'crackling' evident on the left side, which was good news for Dexter, and when he checked his heart, it was beating more regularly. They were reasons to be hopeful, and I left with more tablets for Dexter and feeling a little better about his situation.

After a few months of regular check-ups, Ximo pronounced himself happy to move Dexter to two-monthly appointments, especially when he was able to tell me that, on listening to his lungs, the left lung was clear, no crackling at all. Juliet and I were so happy for Dexter, who continued to enjoy life as normal, though we noticed he walked a little slower and got out of breath if he went too far, or the weather grew too hot. It sounded pretty much like the symptoms I suffer from as a result of my asthma.

The summer seemed to pass so quickly, and soon we were into autumn. As the leaves fell from the trees and the weather grew progressively colder, Dexter's cough seemed to grow worse again and when I took him for one of his regular check-ups, Ximo discovered that he was suffering from a build-up of fluid in his belly. That sounded bad to me, but Ximo told me not to worry and increased Dexter's medication to combat this latest development. The extra medication seemed to have done the trick, because Ximo was pleased to tell me, on our next visit, that the fluid build-up in Dexter's belly had virtually gone. I was so relieved.

Dexter was so used to visiting the vets by now that he positively bounced in through the door when we attended for his regular appointments. He loved the fuss and attention he received from everyone at the practice, where he'd become something of a favourite among the staff. Christmas came and went and we enjoyed a relatively mild winter, which allowed Dexter to spend time with his birds, far more than we would have expected at that time of year. Being winter, we were putting out extra food for the birds, who seemed to be devouring the fat balls as fast as I could replenish them. Dexter certainly didn't mind, as extra food for the birds meant more visits from his feathered friends.

This was the first winter I could remember when we had no snow at all, apart from one quick flurry in February, which didn't even settle long enough for the dogs to go out and play in it.

A lot of my friends on Facebook had been following Dexter's story and his friends at the Facebook group, Bully Lovers and Friends made him their Star of the Day one day, which was so kind of them.

Soon after, we noticed Dexter seemed to be struggling a lot when out for his daily walks, and although he wasn't due for a check-up for another month, I booked him an appointment to see Ximo. After physically examining him, Ximo asked if I could leave Dexter with him for a couple of hours, as he wanted to take some x-rays of his chest and lungs. I agreed and left Dexter with him, returning in the afternoon to collect our boy.

The news wasn't good. Ximo reported to me that though his chest was pretty clear, Dexter's lungs weren't working properly. He took me out back to the treatment area, to the x-ray room, and pulled Dexter's x-rays up. He showed them to me and explained what we were looking at. Dexter's lungs were only operating at between 30 and 40% of their capacity. I was devastated!

"What does it mean for Dexter's future?" I asked.

"Remember what I told you before, Brian. Dexter isn't ill, he's simply getting old and sadly, these are the kind of things that can happen in older dogs. We can't cure the problem, but Dexter is not in any pain, and as long as he's content with life, the best thing you can do is keep him happy. The medication will help, and as long as he's eating and drinking okay and enjoying himself, that's the best we can do for him."

I thanked Ximo, and together, Dexter and I left the surgery. As we reached the car, and I opened the tailgate, expecting to have to help him up, Mr. D. surprised me by leaping up into the car, then turning to face me, with what I was sure was a knowing smile.

"Good boy, Dex," I said, lovingly ruffling the fur on his head. "There's life in the old dog yet, eh? We'll show 'em mate."

I had a big lump in my throat as I said that, and drove home with a heavy heart, but determined, if possible, to give our very special bird-dog one more summer with his birdie friends. I arrived home and walked into the house with Dexter by my side, and as soon as Juliet saw my face, she knew I'd received bad news at the vet.

"What's wrong? What did they say?" she asked.

I told her everything Ximo had told me, and as I finished speaking, she bent down to give Dexter a loving stroke and a cuddle, then looked back at me and agreed with what I'd thought in the car.

"Yes, we'll do everything we can, as long as Dexter's happy. He doesn't have to go for walks if he doesn't feel like it and as long as he's eating and drinking normally, and can go and sit with his birds, that's okay. We know they can't go on forever, and when the time comes, we'll have to make that decision."

I knew that of course, but the odd thing was, we never once thought that Dexter would be the first of our current pack to leave us. He was always the fittest and healthiest of our dogs, never having needed to visit the vet until those lumps appeared a couple of years ago.

For the time being though, Dexter was okay, a bit slower than before, but okay. As the weather grew warmer with the onset of spring, he was able to spend more time down the garden, surrounded by his beloved birdie friends. As spring gave way to the early days of summer, I dared to dream that my wish for Dexter to have one more summer with the birds might just come true, but of course, fate was against us.

One Friday morning in May, Dexter just didn't seem himself, and unusually, he didn't or couldn't get up for breakfast. We thought he might just be tired and left him to sleep in his bed. When the time came for his walk, (and all our dogs somehow know when it's their turn), he didn't raise his head. By now, we were worried, but didn't want to make a snap decision that we might later regret. We decided to see how he was later in the day, and sure enough, soon after lunchtime, Dexter suddenly got up, left his bed and tottered down the garden. He wanted to be near his birds. His walking wasn't great but he made it and sat on his mat for a couple of hours, surrounded by the birds he loved so much.

At feeding time, he ate his food as normal and went out to pee as usual, before taking to his bed for the evening. We went to bed that night hoping he'd be back to normal the next morning. When morning came Dexter looked even worse than he had the previous day. He was unresponsive and didn't look up when either of us spoke to him. we tried everything to coax him to get up and go out to the toilet, all to no avail. His eyes seemed to have lost their sparkle and we both agreed that his time had come.

We had a couple of hours before the vets opened, so we decided that if he was still unresponsive when it reached 8.15 am, we'd make that decision. The hands on the clock moved inexorably round to opening time at the vets and Dexter hadn't improved. Feeling terrible I made the phone call I'd been dreading and the receptionist, one of the girls I knew well, said I could take him down at ten fifteen. That was okay with me, as I wanted to do my usual early morning dog walks first, to try and compose myself, and when I came home with Sheba, Sasha and Dylan, just before 9.45, I had just taken their leads off and hung them up, when I felt a nudge on my leg. Turning and looking down, I was amazed. It was Dexter! This was his normal time for his walk and there he was, large as life, as if to say, *"You're not getting rid of me so easily. Now, can we go for our walk?"* I breathed a massive sigh of relief, and called out to Juliet, who'd been upstairs. She was equally amazed, and came running to see this minor miracle. Before we went for a walk, Dexter went out and did a very long wee, walked to the bottom of the garden, checking out the bird tables and then came in, ready for walkies.

That was a walk like no other. Dexter walked off-lead, very slowly, but obviously enjoying it, and to be honest, I'd never felt closer to him than I did that morning. It wasn't a long walk, it maybe lasted between ten and fifteen minutes, but Mr. D. enjoyed it, even stopping a couple of times for a treat, and doing lots of sniffing at lamp posts, as boy dogs do!

When I got home, Juliet asked me what I was going to do.

"What do you think?" I replied as I picked up the phone and dialled the vets' surgery to cancel the appointment. The receptionist was happy for me and brushed off my apology at cancelling the appointment. As she said, "I can't think of a better reason for cancelling an appointment, Mr. Porter."

We really felt as if we'd been witness to a small miracle and from that day, as Dexter and I walked up the road in the mornings, I grew ever closer to him and we developed an even stronger bond than we'd ever had.

He wasn't eating too well now, so I went out and bought him some of his favourite foods, hot dog sausages and sliced ham, which we mixed in to his food at tea time. He lapped them up. Back in our dog training days, we always used hot dog sausages as rewards for the dogs, and Dexter definitely hadn't forgotten how much he loved them.

Time for walkies Dad

Dexter never fully recovered from that near escape, and we could see he was struggling to walk on some days. It was now the beginning of June, and he'd at least made it to the summer.

He was now spending most of the day at the bottom of the garden, either lying in the sun, or sitting under the bird table with his little friends around him. Three weeks after that day when I cancelled the appointment, Dexter suddenly went downhill, fast. On the Friday, he again showed an unwillingness to get out of his bed, and didn't get up for his breakfast. I fed him a few pieces of hot dog sausage and a couple of slices of ham by hand, and we didn't even try to make him get up to go for a walk.

I think both Juliet and I knew that this time, if he couldn't get up, then we weren't going to have a choice. We had to give him a chance though, so agreed to give him 24 hours to see if it made a difference. At tea time I had to feed him by hand again, three slices of ham and two large chopped hot dog sausages. He hadn't moved all day and we knew his time was running out. That night, I was happy for him when his best friend, Muttley got into bed with him, cuddled up to him and stayed there with him all night. He wasn't alone on his last night. I know that, because I couldn't sleep and kept coming downstairs to check on him. Both Juliet and I had hoped that one night he would just go to sleep and not wake up, but our Dexter was too strong and stubborn-minded for that. I spent most of that night downstairs, in the kitchen stroking him and Muttley as they slept, snuggled up as if it was just another regular night. I knew it wasn't and my heart ached for them both, these two best friends who life was about to play a cruel trick on.

Dexter's last night, with Muttley

Next morning, Dexter didn't get up, he didn't move, and he looked lifeless. Although he managed to take a few pieces of hot dog sausage from my hand, we knew that the reprieve he'd been granted three weeks earlier was at an end. This time, though it broke our hearts to admit it, it was time for Dexter to cross the Rainbow Bridge.

Once again, at 8.15 am, I called the vets. Shannon, the receptionist couldn't have been more helpful and sympathetic. She went away to check and came back and told me I could take Dexter in right away, and that Ximo would be there for me. I was so relieved it was going to be Ximo, rather than someone Dexter didn't know.

Juliet helped me to carry poor Dexter to the car and we gently laid him on the mattress in the back. She tearfully said her goodbyes to Mr. D. and I set off on the worst journey of my life, fighting back the tears as I drove. When I arrived I didn't bother with the car park. I pulled up right outside the front door, and two of the girls immediately came out to the car with a dog stretcher and gently lifted Dexter into it, and carried him inside, straight into the consulting room.

Once there, they lifted him, oh so gently from the stretcher and laid him carefully on his side on the consulting table. Each of them gave him a stroke before leaving me with him for a minute, until Ximo came into the room accompanied by Helen, one of the practice nurses. As always, Ximo reached out and shook my hand, but this time he went one further, putting his arms around my shoulders and giving me a man hug. We didn't need words at that time. He proceeded to examine Dexter, and after a couple of minutes, he looked up at me and said,

"Brian, Dexter's left lung has stopped working altogether. I could possibly bring him round and give him another couple of weeks."

"But if you did, Ximo, would he be able to walk, or play, or even go down the garden to be with his birdie mates?"

Ximo just shook his head. After a pause he said, "Brian, the final decision is yours."

I looked at my beautiful Dexter, lying there, unmoving and dwindling away before my eyes and I knew he'd had enough. I knew I had to be strong for both of us.

"Let's give him some peace, some rest, Ximo. He's earned it."

Ximo nodded and said, "We'll leave you alone with him for a couple of minutes, while we get the injection ready."

With that, he and Helen left the room and Dexter and I were alone together, for what I knew was going to be the last time, our final moments together. I leaned down close to him and spoke softly to him, hoping he could hear me and understand what I was saying. I told him I loved him, that his Mum loved him as well as all the doggies and all his lovely birds. I told him he was the best dog in the world and that I was sorry we had to say goodbye, but that we'd never forget him. I got rather choked up at that point and then, something incredible happened.

Dexter, my lovely, beautiful, faithful Dexter, lifted his head from the table, looked me right in the eye, and gave me a great big, wet, doggie kiss. I couldn't believe it. I just broke down, and the tears flowed. As if that wasn't enough, a few seconds later, he did it again. Where he got the strength from to do that, I'll never know, but it was as if he was saying thank you, or goodbye, or something extremely profound that I could only guess at. Maybe he was telling me to look after the birds for him, I just don't know.

When Ximo came back into the room, he put a hand on my shoulder and asked if I wanted some more time with Dexter.

I managed to say, "No it's okay. We've said our goodbyes," and the tears came again.

"I really don't want to do this, Brian," he said, and I replied, "I know, but he needs to rest now, Ximo. Please, let him rest."

Ximo nodded, got me to sign the consent form, and quickly shaved the fur from Dexter's paw, and then, as I held his head, and lovingly stroked him, Ximo gave him the injection. He almost had tears in his eyes as he did it. It was over in seconds. I almost felt the life leaving his body and asked, "Has he gone?"

Ximo confirmed that Dexter had passed away and said he and Helen would leave me and Dexter together for a while.

"Take as long as you like," he said. "There's no rush, and when you're ready, come through the back and we'll let you out that way so you won't have to walk through the waiting room."

He was so incredibly caring, and I think he loved Dexter almost as much as me. He'd treated him so well throughout his illness and did everything he could for him, and for that, Juliet and I will always be grateful.

I stayed with Dexter for about ten or fifteen minutes, talking softly to him, even though I knew he'd gone, his little doggie soul was already winging its way to doggie heaven. I promised him I'd take care of the birds, and look after his best pal, Muttley, who really depended on Dexter, and then Ximo knocked on the door and he and Helen came back into the room.

"Don't worry about anything, Brian, we'll take good care of him," Ximo said. "Do you know whether you want his ashes back? Don't decide now, let us know by Monday, and don't worry about the bill. You're insured anyway. We can sort that out when you're ready."

All I could do was say thank you to everyone, and one of the girls quietly let me out the back door, after giving me a big hug. I sat in the car for about five minutes, composing myself, and then rang Juliet.

"Dexter's gone," was all I managed, before the tears started again.

"Don't say any more," Juliet said, "and don't set off in the car until you're ready."

It was twenty minutes later when I walked in through the back door and Juliet greeted me with a hug, and we sort of had a joint crying session, as we let our emotions out. It was much later in the day that I was able to tell her about Dexter's last act, his kisses as he lay on the table, and that made her cry some more.

We knew we'd miss our bird-dog, but so too would Muttley, his best doggie friend, as well as the other dogs, but it was Muttley who was hardest hit by Dexter's passing. He'd lost his sleep partner, and it took him a few weeks to realise that Dexter wasn't coming home.

We had one more decision to make and Juliet, rightly, made

the decision not to have Dexter's ashes returned, as she knew she'd only get upset every time she walked past the urn, or jar.

Instead we came up with a very special way of honouring and remembering our very special bird-dog. Read the next chapter to see how Dexter's story really ends.

14

DEXTER'S MEMORIAL GARDEN

DEXTER WAS GONE, passed over the Rainbow Bridge to that special place we call Dog Heaven, where I hope he'll make lots of doggie pals and be surrounded by more birds than he ever knew existed down here on earth.

As I mentioned at the end of the previous chapter, Juliet and I decided not to have Dexter's ashes returned. I agreed with Juliet that we'd find it too upsetting to have to walk past an urn with his ashes in time and again, every day.

However, after a little thinking, I came up with what Juliet agreed was a great and a fitting way to commemorate the life of Dexter the Bird Dog. I decided to completely redesign the area at the bottom of our back garden to create a haven for Dexter's feathered friends, and which would be a permanent memorial to Dexter.

We already had two bird tables, one of which, the large one, was bought for us as a wedding present by Juliet's son, Robert. The second, smaller one, however, was getting on in years and was in sore need of replacing. Now was the time to do it. In fact, as part of my plan for what quickly became known as

'Dexter's Garden' I ordered not one but two new bird tables. While waiting for them to arrive, I also ordered two engraved brass plaques, inscribed with different wording which commemorated Dexter and which would be fixed to the new tables when they arrived.

I was amazed when the first table arrived within 24 hours of being ordered, (good old Amazon Prime), and I set to work assembling it to have it ready when the plaque arrived. It looked really nice and to give it a professional finish, I went out and bought some good quality wood stain and treated it with three coats, by which time it looked terrific, a worthy remembrance of our boy. The plaque arrived a few days later and I fixed it to the table, and put it to one side in the garden as I wasn't putting it in its final position until the other table arrived and I'd bought the new plants and tubs I needed to complete the garden.

The first table

While the garden was being slowly put together, Juliet and I were extremely touched by the reaction we received to Dexter's loss. Within hours of me announcing his passing on Facebook, we were surprised by a knock on the door. I answered it to a man holding a beautiful, big bouquet of flowers. A friend of mine on Facebook, Kath Bradbury, had seen my announcement and immediately organised the delivery of this gorgeous bouquet in Dexter's memory. She followed it up a few days later when we received a beautiful card and a photo of Dexter in a transparent heart, also from Kath, which she'd posted to us on the day of his death. Her kindness was overwhelming at such a time.

From Dexter's friends and admirers

Meanwhile, another friend, my fellow author, Linda Lindsay, (aka Linda Meredith), saw the news and also organised a tribute to Dexter which was delivered to us a few days later. That was so kind and thoughtful and we were touched again by her gesture of remembrance for Dexter.

We were especially touched to receive a condolence card from our vet, which even included a pack of Forget-Me-Not seeds to plant in remembrance of Dexter. They were definitely destined for his memorial garden.

Meanwhile, the second new table was here, assembled and primed with wood stain. Like the first one, this was stored to one side until I was ready to place the two tables in their positions. I made a few trips to various shops to purchase plants (and planters), compost and topsoil for the garden. I enjoyed selecting plants that the birds wouldn't peck at and destroy, and tried to limit my choices to perennials that would grow year after year. On one trip to the shops, while looking at plants, I came across some very attractive, tall planters, and I thought they would be ideal for Dexter's garden, so they were added to my shopping trolley.

Table 2

Next came a few solar-powered miners' lanterns, the crackle ball type, that constantly change colour through the night, some solar-powered dragonflies, and a couple of shepherd's lanterns.

Once the plants had been planted and fed and watered for a couple of weeks to make sure none were about to die, (none did), I finally felt ready to complete work on the garden. Luckily, a friend of mine had just begun work on creating a new, hand-made fence down one side of the garden and I asked him to make the first panel so it provided a nice backdrop for Dexter's memorial. Two final plaques were ordered and placed in one of the planters, and on the large bird table, and we were ready. I say we, because without Juliet's help, I'd never have been able to manhandle all the pots and planters to the bottom of the garden by myself.

So finally, six weeks after losing our beautiful boy, Dexter's

Memorial Garden was complete, with new bird tables, beautiful plants and colourful lights to illuminate the darkness. I know it might sound silly to some people, but I decided to hold an 'Official Opening Ceremony', the very special guest list comprising Juliet and our ten remaining dogs, who probably wondered what they'd been called out for.

I made a short speech, "It's my great pleasure to dedicate this memorial garden to the memory of our much loved and very much missed friend, Dexter, our very special bird-dog. Mr. D., if you're looking down on us from your new home at the Rainbow Bridge, I hope you like your own special memorial garden. I've tried to do you proud. We still love you, and we'll always miss you. Sleep soundly little friend, and Dexter's Memorial Garden is now officially open, all birds welcome."

There's not a lot more to tell you. Dexter's life, from the

time we adopted him, was very much a happy one and we hope he knew how much he was loved and wanted. It's so sad that our dogs' lives are so short compared to ours, but if we can believe what we're told, that one dog year is equal to seven of ours, then that means he was 84 in dog years when he left us, and that's not a bad age, I suppose.

Thank you to you all for reading his story. I hope you enjoyed it and will maybe consider reading some more of the books in the series.

Rest in peace, Dexter. Love you always.

Brian L Porter

Dear reader,

We hope you enjoyed reading *Remembering Dexter*. Please take a moment to leave a review, even if it's a short one. Your opinion is important to us.

Discover more books by Brian L Porter at

https://www.nextchapter.pub/authors/brian-porter-mystery-author-liverpool-united-kingdom

Want to know when one of our books is free or discounted? Join the newsletter at

http://eepurl.com/bqqB3H

Best regards,

Brian L Porter and the Next Chapter Team

ABOUT THE AUTHOR

Brian L Porter is an award-winning, bestselling author, whose books have regularly topped the Amazon Best Selling charts. Writing as Brian, he has won a Best Author Award, and his mystery/thrillers have picked up Best Thriller and Best Mystery Awards. The third book in his Mersey Mystery series, *A Mersey Maiden* won The Best Book We've Read all Year Award, 2018, from Readfree.ly. In addition, *Cassie's Tale* was the runner-up in the 2018 Top 50 Best Indie Books of the year, at the same time winning the Non-fiction category, and *A Very Mersey Murder* finished in 5th place in the same awards, while also winning the Best Mystery Novel Award.

When it comes to dogs and dog rescue, he is passionate about the subject and his three previous dog rescue books have been hugely successful. *Sasha: A Very Special Dog Tale of a Very Special Epi-Dog* is now an award-winning international bestseller and *Sheba: From Hell to Happiness* is also a UK Bestseller and an award winner too. *Cassie's Tale*, the third book in the series, also followed Sasha and Sheba in winning the Critters.org, (formerly Preditors and Editors), annual Best Non-fiction award, 2018, and there are sure to be more to follow. The fourth book in the series, Penny the Railway Pup immediately became a bestselling new release and recently a number one bestseller in Australia.

While available to preorder on Amazon, *Remembering Dexter* became a UK bestseller. Dexter would be proud of that.

Writing as Harry Porter his children's books have achieved bestselling rankings on Amazon in the USA and UK and Italy

In addition, his third incarnation as romantic poet Juan Pablo Jalisco has brought international recognition with his collected works, *Of Aztecs and Conquistadors* topping the bestselling charts in the USA, UK and Canada.

Brian lives with his wife, eldest step-daughter and of course, Sasha and the rest of his wonderful pack of ten rescued dogs, in the North of England.

A Mersey Killing and the subsequent books in his Mersey Mystery series have already been optioned for adaptation as a TV series, in addition to his other novels, all of which have been signed by ThunderBall Films in a movie franchise deal.

See Brian's website at http://www.brianlporter.co.uk

You can find the Rescue Dog series at http://viewbook.at/rescuedogs

Sasha has her own Facebook page, which contains information about all the dogs, at Sasha the Wagging Tail of England https://www.facebook.com/groups/270003923193039/

And all the Mersey Mystery series is at http://getbook.at/MerseyMysteries

Brian's blog is at https://sashaandharry.blogspot.com/

You can find all his books by visiting his author page at Amazon

The Award-winning Rescue Dog series

OTHER BOOKS BY THE AUTHOR

Dog Rescue Series

Sasha – A Very Special Dog Tale of a Very Special Epi-Dog

Sheba: From Hell to Happiness

Cassie's Tale

Penny the Railway Pup

Remembering Dexter

Dylan - Bedlington Blue (Coming soon)

Thrillers by Brian L Porter

A Study in Red - The Secret Journal of Jack the Ripper

Legacy of the Ripper

Requiem for the Ripper

Pestilence

Purple Death

Behind Closed Doors

Avenue of the Dead

The Nemesis Cell

Kiss of Life

The Mersey Mystery Series

A Mersey Killing (Amazon bestseller)

All Saints, Murder on the Mersey

A Mersey Maiden

A Mersey Mariner

A Very Mersey Murder

Last Train to Lime Street

The Mersey Monastery Murders

A Liverpool Lullaby (Coming in 2020)

Short Story Collections

After Armageddon (Amazon bestseller)

Remembrance Poetry

Lest We Forget (Amazon bestseller)

Children's books as Harry Porter

Wolf (Amazon bestseller)

Alistair the Alligator, (Illustrated by Sharon Lewis) (Amazon bestseller)

Charlie the Caterpillar (Illustrated by Bonnie Pelton) (Amazon bestseller)

As Juan Pablo Jalisco

Of Aztecs and Conquistadors (Amazon bestseller)

Love from all of us, Dexter too!

REMEMBERING DEXTER
Memories of a very special bird-loving dog

Discarded like a piece of rubbish.
Dexter was rescued by the author and found a unique fulfilment in his life.
He loved and protected the birds who came to feed in 'his' garden every day.
This is his story.

You might also like:

Fully Staffed by Linda A. Meredith

To read the first chapter for free go to:
https://www.nextchapter.pub/books/fully-staffed

Remembering Dexter
ISBN: 978-4-86751-312-5

Published by
Next Chapter
1-60-20 Minami-Otsuka
170-0005 Toshima-Ku, Tokyo
+818035793528

29th June 2021